D0434488

The Dragon Roars Again

WALES' JOURNEY TO EURO 2016

'An excellent contribution to Welsh football literature.
I have met and spoken with Jamie on a number of
occasions during the campaign and his support and
enthusiasm for Welsh football is clear.'

Chris Coleman

'A totally different account of Wales' journey.
A very good book from a promising new writer who
seems to have a future in the industry.'

Trefor Lloyd Hughes

'An excellent account of Wales' journey to Euro 2016.
Taking into account all the heartbreak of years gone by and
how it has defined Wales as a footballing nation is no mean
feat. Jamie has a bright future ahead of him.'

Gary Pritchard

'A superbly researched book, full of in-depth information
on Wales' return to the pinnacle of football from the people
who made it possible. An incredible story, very well told.'

Roger Speed

'An achievement to redefine Welsh football told by the
people that made the dream a reality. A comprehensive and
passion-filled account of what made qualification possible.'

Mark Pitman

The Dragon
Roars Again

WALES' JOURNEY
TO EURO 2016

JAMIE THOMAS

LLYFRGELLOEDD SIR DDINBYCH	
C46 0000 0555 771	
Askews & Holts	14-Jun-2016
796.3340942ᶟᵍ	£9.99
DE	

First impression: 2016

© Copyright Jamie Thomas and Y Lolfa Cyf., 2016

The contents of this book are subject to copyright, and may
not be reproduced by any means, mechanical or electronic,
without the prior, written consent of the publishers.

The publishers wish to acknowledge the support of
Cyngor Llyfrau Cymru

Photographs: David Rawcliffe, Propaganda Photo
Cover design: Y Lolfa

ISBN: 978 1 78461 243 6

Published and printed in Wales
on paper from well-maintained forests by
Y Lolfa Cyf., Talybont, Ceredigion SY24 5HE
website www.ylolfa.com
e-mail ylolfa@ylolfa.com
tel 01970 832 304
fax 832 782

ACKNOWLEDGMENTS

THE PURPOSE OF this book is to contribute to a conversation about Welsh football – I hope I've achieved that in some way – but first I'd like to thank the people that have contributed their own time and insights to help me on my way to putting this all together.

I'd like to start with Graham Hunter; he gave me the inspiration to write this book and has been a very big help to me, so thanks chief!

A huge thanks to the publishers Y Lolfa and Lefi Gruffudd who supported me all the way – when a boy in his early twenties approaches you with no publishing experience and tells you he wants to write about the hottest sporting topic in the country, you've got to have guts to say yes.

The FAW need to be thanked immensely too, no more so than the President at the time, Trefor Lloyd Hughes, who was an immense help to me. I've probably become the bane of Peter Barnes and Ian Gwyn Hughes' lives over the past year or so, nagging them for one thing or another, a big thank you goes to both of them. Thanks to Mark Evans, Rob Dowling, CEO Jonathan Ford for their immense efforts. Thank you to the press officers at the clubs I've been in contact with, who have been very accommodating. Michael Benson, you too pal.

I cannot thank the contributors enough. All of the players I've spoken to have been amazingly helpful; particularly Wayne Hennessey who was my first interviewee from the current squad. Jonny Williams, Owain Fôn Williams, Emyr Huws, Sam Vokes, James Chester, Neil Taylor, Ashley Williams, Joe Ledley, Simon Church, Ben Davies, Jack Collison, Tyler Roberts, the whole squad, they've been superb! Chris Whitley, Gus Williams – fantastic, enthusiastic and exceptionally helpful. Osian Roberts has been brilliant too, as well as the man who is going to lead the squad to big things in France, Chris Coleman – a massive thanks to them both of course. Kit Symons, Ian

Mitchell, Raymond Verheijen and Damian Roden all gave so much of their time to speak to me, which I'm immensely grateful for.

The guys in the media, Mark Pitman, Chris Wathan, Andrew Gwilym, Rob Phillips, Phil Blanche, Dafydd Pritchard, Dylan Ebenezer and Gary Pritchard contributed readily and were always offering a helping hand. Geraint Ellis at Bangor University too, thank you very much mate!

The supporters I've spoken to have been brilliant; Owain Roberts, Gareth Bennett, Mikey Peters and Aiden Williams especially – travelling with me to games and discussing them with me for weeks afterwards for this book – they've certainly been an immense help. All of my friends and family have been great too, invaluable shoulders to lean on for advice, especially Laura – love you dweeb, and an honourable mention has to go to my mum, of course! Seth Burkett, you've been great too, man!

Thank you very much to the Speed family as well, for giving me their blessing to write about the legend himself, Gary Speed; I hope I've done that incredible man, and the enormous part he played in the Welsh football story, some small justice. John Martin, Don Murray, Matty Jones, you guys have been invaluably helpful too and I will never forget it, as well as all of the people I spoke to regarding Speed's career: Cledwyn Ashford, Sam Allardyce, Howard Wilkinson, Shay Given, Joe Royle, John Carver, Andy Melville, Jason Koumas, Neville Southall, Steve Williams, Tony Quaglia, Iwan Roberts, Kevin Ratcliffe, thank you all very much for helping me with my research. Mickey Thomas and Joey Jones too, they helped me immensely in my research, thank you very much guys!

Finally, because I promised they'd always make the acknowledgements. Thanks to Beth and Laura, for being Beth and Laura!

Contents

PART 1

'Always the Bridesmaid, never the Bride'

JOEY JONES, WALES, 1975–86

Chapter 1

Dodgy decisions and missed opportunities – Wales after Pelé and 1958

'I don't think it was psychological that we were going
to fail, but it is very difficult to put your finger on;
things just never went our way'

Joey Jones, Wales, 1975–86

It took a stunning goal from a youthful Pelé to send Wales packing from their first and only FIFA World Cup finals on 19 June 1958, in a game that set Brazil on the path to their first world title. And after that tournament in Sweden it would be another 58 years before Wales would qualify for a second major international tournament.

Having squandered numerous opportunities to accomplish the feat, Wales at last qualified for the finals of the 2016 UEFA European Championships in France on 10 October 2015. There were a few heart-in-mouth moments in this campaign alone, for sure. Falling behind in Andorra; under the cosh away at Belgium; first versus second in Haifa – almost on a game-by-game basis there were moments for most supporters when they felt it would all go wrong.

Anyone not Welsh reading this may be wondering: 'Why write this book? What's the big deal? It's only one tournament.' Yes, it is just one tournament, but it's the story behind it that makes it such an exceptional achievement. I remember speaking to broadcaster Mal Pope back in 2014 about a documentary he was working on called *Jack to a King: The Swansea Story* – looking in depth at the tale behind Swansea City Football Club's historic, ten-year rise from the very bottom of the Football League to the Barclays Premier League. I interviewed Mal about the documentary while at university and the one thing he kept repeating during the interview was how he believed it was a Hollywood story that needed to be told. Everything that could have gone wrong with that club, on the way to the top, went wrong. And yet they still got there. They still achieved what history would have suggested was impossible. Wales' story in this instance is exactly the same.

Despite the fact Wales made it to the World Cup finals in 1958 and performed very well at the tournament, they were with all due respect exceptionally lucky to get there. Wales finished second in their 1958 qualifying group, so were officially out of the competition. It took a historical twist of fate for them to make it to Sweden. Amid a turbulent political situation in the Middle East, Israel were proclaimed winners of their group by default after each of their opponents either refused to play them at all, or refused to play them in Israel. FIFA did not want any team to go through without playing a game, so drew the names of all the second-placed UEFA teams out of a hat, proposing a two-legged play-off against Israel for a spot at the tournament. Belgium were drawn out first but refused to participate. Wales were drawn out next and agreed to the play-off against Israel, winning 4–0 on aggregate.

Since 1958, as Mal described with Swansea City, everything that could have gone wrong for Wales in their qualification campaigns did go wrong, and then some. And you cannot understand why the Euro 2016 qualification means so much to Wales fans without understanding what has come and gone before it.

Throughout the remainder of the 20th century, Wales came within touching distance of reaching a major tournament finals on a number of occasions. Euro '76 was the first example. This Wales team has since been labelled 'the forgotten XI', as no-one mentions this side's success, perhaps because the tournament format was different to what we would today consider to be orthodox. The qualifying round for Euro '76 consisted of 32 teams split into eight groups, with the last 16 going into a knock-out round and the final tournament consisting of just four teams. Wales reached the last eight and lost 3–1 to Yugoslavia, who went on to play in the final tournament against Czechoslovakia, The Netherlands and West Germany. Wales made it out of the group phase, but didn't reach the final tournament. A veil has been drawn over this particular qualification campaign, which is unfortunate because this Wales team went further than any other Wales team between 1958 and 2016.

Joey Jones, a left-back who made 72 appearances for Wales between 1975 and 1986, summarised Wales' qualifying struggles. 'It did bother us,' says Jones, 'because we were trying desperately hard to qualify, for our country more than ourselves. We qualified for '76 under the old rules with the Euros, back with Mike Smith, but as far as the World Cup goes we were always the bridesmaid, and never the bride.'

Qualification for the World Cup in 1978 was another one of those 'bridesmaid' occasions – an infamous campaign with two games against Scotland proving to be Wales' undoing. Wales lost the opening game of their group at Hampden Park 1–0, courtesy of an own goal by Ian Evans. According to Welsh midfielder Mickey Thomas, who started that game, Wales were 'very unlucky to lose that game 1–0, despite giving a really good performance'. Wales showed superb home form in the second game of the group, as they beat Czechoslovakia 3–0 at Wrexham. The visitors were European Champions at the time and that defeat was only their second loss in 26 games, which was a testament to Wales' confidence at The Racecourse.

The next game, at home to Scotland, will live long in the memory of every Wales fan because of an incident involving Scottish forward Joe Jordan in the 78th minute. Following crowd trouble at Ninian Park during Wales' Euro '76 play-off with Yugoslavia the previous year, this game, like the one before it, could not be held at Ninian Park as a punishment to Wales. Wales could have played the game in Wrexham, and it would have made sense given the great record Wales had there, but the Football Association of Wales decided to stage the match at Anfield to raise more money from the stadium's bigger capacity. The FAW got its wish in that sense as a capacity crowd packed the stands, but some of the Scottish players told the media that they were very happy to be playing what was essentially the group decider at Anfield. They knew how good Wales were at The Racecourse, and that more Scottish fans would make the shorter trip to Liverpool.

Regardless of the change of venue, what ultimately cost Wales was a horrific refereeing decision. Scotland were awarded a penalty in the 78th minute for handball – an offence committed in the eyes of the referee by Wales centre-back Dave Jones, when in fact Jordan had blatantly handled the ball. Don Masson tucked away the penalty, before Kenny Dalglish scored to seal the two points and qualification to the 1978 World Cup for Scotland. Wales had a game left in the group after that, a 1–0 defeat away to Czechoslovakia, but by that time the group had been tied up. Joe Jordan has said previously that he cannot cross the River Severn now without receiving abuse from the Welsh, but it was the referee's decision in that game at Anfield against Scotland that cost Wales their hopes of qualification.

The 1980s saw Wales develop world-class stars in volume, such as Ian Rush, Neville Southall, Mark Hughes and Kevin Ratcliffe and, again, the side came desperately close to qualifying for a couple of tournaments in that decade. Ratcliffe, captaining the side for many of his 59 caps, describes his side's qualifying struggles succinctly: 'It was the one thing missing from my CV, really, qualifying for a major international championship. You know, it was very difficult but we came close. Like always, we were unfortunate, because one thing or another always went wrong, people or players were missing, a depleted squad… we had the old scenario of round pegs in square holes.'

Some took the stance that the Welsh squad didn't have the

necessary depth to best complement their top players, as a lot of the squad plied their trade in the lower leagues. If you speak to any of the top talent that was in that squad, however, they will say that it wasn't the lower league players that let them down. Neville Southall gets particularly worked up about this topic: 'People don't realise how good these players were,' he says. 'To be able to turn around in a few days and learn a totally different way of playing, a totally new level... what they did was incredible, but they'd never get any praise for it. It was always "Oh Wales didn't have enough good players," which was rubbish. People looked down on them, but they should have been looking up to them and saying how extraordinary they were.' One such example would be Alan Knill, who in 1988 turned out for third division Bury before being asked to mark Marco van Basten when Wales played Holland. It was an almost impossible task, but Knill and the many other players from the lower leagues performed their duties to a very high standard.

Wales also fell at the last hurdle of qualifying for a major tournament in 1984 and 1986. The most frustrating thing, according to some of the squad, was that Wales had no problem performing at their best against the bigger teams, but really struggled to get going against the lesser sides. 'Wales teams seem to always be the underdog,' explains Southall, 'so when we came across teams like Iceland and the Faroe Islands we found it more of a struggle. But if we played Spain, Italy, Germany, then we'd all be up for it, because we knew we were the underdogs in the scenario. Sometimes it's easier to play against big teams than it is to play against smaller teams.'

Losing 1–0 away to Iceland in the first game of the 1986 World Cup campaign made qualification incredibly difficult. Wales went to Spain for the second fixture and were brushed aside 3–0. The Dragons did turn it around, winning their next three – against Iceland at home, Scotland away and an incredible 3–0 win against Spain at home – before once again it all came down to a decisive game against Scotland, this time at

Ninian Park. The 1–1 draw wasn't enough for Wales to progress to the final tournament, but the game will be remembered less for this fact than for the death of legendary Scottish manager Jock Stein. It was a tragic turn of events and, according to those on the Scottish bench, something that came completely out of the blue, as Stein could still be seen shouting at coaches and players right until the final whistle when he collapsed to his knees and passed away, having failed to take medication to treat his heart muscle disease. Football doesn't matter at times like that.

The 1994 World Cup was the last time in the 20th century that Wales would go close to qualifying for a major tournament finals. In contrast to previous years, Wales did very well against the lesser teams in the group, but ultimately lost the chance of qualification after two disappointing results against a very good Romania side – a 5–1 loss away and an infamous 2–1 defeat at home in the final group game. 'We didn't quite have the right balance in the squad,' says Southall. 'We missed an outstanding midfield player. We had great midfielders, but we didn't have a Gazza, a Souness, or a Hagi, and I think that was the main difference. Up front we weren't bad; defensively we weren't bad; we were good in midfield, but creatively I think we just missed something.' Kevin Ratcliffe went further, adding if that team had been able to field Aaron Ramsey – the type of midfielder many felt Wales were missing – alongside Gary Speed, Ryan Giggs, Ian Rush and Mark Hughes, then they would have qualified on multiple occasions.

The other fixtures in the group went fairly well, but the games against Romania cost Wales the group. In the final game at Cardiff Arms Park, Gheorghe Hagi, considered by many to be one of the best attacking midfielders in the world at the time, put the Romanians ahead after half an hour, before Dean Saunders levelled on the hour mark for Wales. Moments later Gary Speed was tripped inside the area and Wales were awarded a penalty. Paul Bodin stepped up to take it but missed – an absolute sucker-punch to Wales' qualification chances.

Southall, however, is quick to take the blame from Bodin: 'The pressure on him was enormous and, let's be fair, he only missed by an inch and he's got loads of grief. I always hear people picking on the fact that he missed it but it was my fault for Hagi's goal, and I don't get anywhere near the amount of stick that Bodin did. He was brave enough to take a penalty – there wasn't a big queue for it.'

Romania went on to score again and won the game 2–1. Yet again Wales had fallen at the crucial stage – the story of their fortunes between 1958 and 2016. But there was a greater tragedy in this match, as a member of the crowd died after being hit in the chest by a projectile. Going to a football match to support your country and not making it home, it puts everything into perspective.

CHAPTER 2

Sparky, Tosh and a changing of the guard – Euro 2004 and the next generation

'You can't do everything, but Sparky definitely took the set-up forward. Afterwards, I think Tosh did see a longer-term plan, looking beyond merely the next campaign.'

CHRIS WATHAN, WALES ONLINE

FOLLOWING THE RELATIVE success of the 1994 qualifying campaign, Wales fans were full of optimism. Aside from two tough results against Romania, who went on to reach the quarter-finals of USA '94, the campaign had been a great success, with many expecting the future to be very bright. The senior players in that squad played on for a few more years, and its younger members only got better. The likes of Gary Speed and Ryan Giggs were taking British football by storm, so it was reasonable to expect that the squad would have continued to raise the bar, possibly qualifying for a tournament before the turn of the millennium. Needless to say, it didn't happen. For one reason or another, the light started to fade for Wales after that Romania game.

Terry Yorath's departure as manager after the infamous Romania defeat in 1993 was followed by John Toshack's brief one-game tenure. Mike Smith then led the team for 18 months, and Bobby Gould was the man in charge for more or less the rest of the decade. After a 4–0 thrashing by Italy in Bologna in June 1999, however, Gould handed in his resignation and suggested that Neville Southall and Mark Hughes should apply for the job. Both took temporary charge of Wales while the

FAW decided who would take the team forward permanently, settling eventually on Hughes. Southall learned of his fate on the radio but was happy for his former teammate. 'Sparky had his own people he had to bring in, which is fair enough,' he says. 'He changed a lot in Welsh football and, again because he's not flamboyant, I don't think he got the credit he deserved. Gouldy came in and started things moving in lots of ways, particularly logistically with hotels, travelling and so on, but Sparky came in and built further on that, bringing a bit of Manchester United to Wales and you could see the impact that had on the players.'

The idea was simple: give the players a Premier League environment and they will respond like Premier League players. This modernisation of the logistical side was exceptionally important at a time when Wales were struggling for results. Hughes recognised this and fought tooth and nail to modernise things to the best of his ability, while navigating the tight budgets that came with Wales' relative lack of success at the time.

The first campaign for which Hughes was entirely responsible was qualification for the 2002 World Cup. Results on the pitch were hard to come by but, nonetheless, the likes of Andy Melville, Jason Koumas, Matty Jones and Tony Quaglia all spoke highly of Hughes' ambition to change the set-up, praising the team spirit he created within the squad as one of the focal points of his success. Melville, one of Wales' most experienced players under Hughes, said: 'He was very good, very impressive. He got everything organised and took our set-up to the next level. We started to work more as a unit defensively, we were doing it constantly while we were away together, and we got our rewards in the end. We were turning losses into draws to start with, then draws into wins.'

The turnaround didn't happen straight away, though, as Hughes' side went on a record run of 12 games without a win, consisting of six draws and six losses from March 2000 to September 2001. There were positive signs to be taken from that run, as four of the six losses came in the opening four games, and after that the run consisted of six draws and two losses. Nothing to shout about, perhaps, but steps in the right direction were being taken. Quaglia, Mark Hughes' head of logistics, notes that the 0–0 draw with Poland in Warsaw, halfway into the 12-game winless run, was a big turning point for Hughes. 'All that Mark had worked for started to come together,' he says, '... getting to know the players, understanding their mind-sets and their capabilities.'

The winless streak stopped at 12 as Wales knocked off Belarus 1–0 in Cardiff, and from then on things drastically improved. Draws against Argentina, Czech Republic and Croatia, as well as a famous friendly win against Germany, meant that Wales were going into their Euro 2004 qualifying campaign in excellent form; a significant turnaround from the team that couldn't beat Armenia at home 12 months before. There was a sense that it was all building towards something, but Wales fans had seen their hopes dashed before.

Group draws have historically been pretty difficult for the Welsh. A consequence of their lack of success is their low seeding, and the draw for Euro 2004 qualifying was no exception as Hughes' men were the fourth seeds in a five-team group. When you factor in the qualifying situation then, where only the top team qualified automatically and the second-placed team went into the play-offs (as opposed to now where two teams qualify and the third goes into a play-off), a fourth-seed nation was going to have to be incredibly lucky, perform exceptionally well, or both, to progress to the final tournament. The quality within Wales' squad at the time counted in their favour, however; it was one of the most balanced Wales squads ever. There was a good mix of top talent with the likes of Giggs and Speed, great young players such as Simon Davies, Craig Bellamy and Jason Koumas, as well as the experienced heads of Andy Melville, John Hartson and Mark Pembridge.

Matty Jones notes how this squad had something it'd previously been missing. 'We've always had the top-class individuals,' he says, 'but we've struggled for the glue to hold that together within the squad, in terms of depth. This was the first squad where we had a good balance from front to back and a good mix of quality.' This side also shared the attributes of previous ones, with players from the lower leagues able to come in and perform exceptionally well when required. 'You still had those players who stepped up when it came to Wales,' says Wales Online journalist Chris Wathan, 'such as Danny Gabbidon, who was excellent in that campaign but was still playing in the English third tier when he was marking the likes of Alessandro Del Piero, which is incredible.'

As important as it is to get a kind group, the order in which you face your opponents can be crucial too – you don't want to play the top seeds away from home in your first game, for example. Wales' opening two fixtures were away against Finland, the team seeded directly above Wales, followed by the top seeds, Italy, in Cardiff. The first game was especially crucial. Being at home Finland would have expected a win, whereas Wales were in their best form for a while, which was reflected by the number of supporters that travelled out there – they obviously sensed the opportunity. Wales won the game 2–0, which was a huge sign of how far this team had come, with the team capitalising on the positive momentum they had been able to build. Previously under Hughes, Wales had struggled somewhat away from home, even in friendlies, so to go and get such a big result in this game was key in building confidence for the remainder of the campaign.

The home game against Italy was just one of those games that everyone gets excited for, something that takes care of itself because the occasion motivates everyone to perform. It was the perfect time to play Italy, too. They weren't the same team they had been a couple of years before when they had reached the final of Euro 2000. There were rumours of infighting among the Italian players. So if Wales were ever going to beat Italy, it was going to be now. The FAW sensed the opportunity, too, with bands performing on the pitch, legends like John Charles presenting before the game, and a sell-out crowd. Wales dominated the match, taking the lead after 11 minutes through Simon Davies before being pegged back to 1–1 by an Alessandro Del Piero goal. But then Craig Bellamy scored with 20 minutes to go, sealing arguably Wales' most significant competitive victory for over a decade. Andy Melville was very proud of his teammates after such a momentous victory. 'These games always have plusses and minuses,' says Melville. 'On the plus side you're always going to go into them as motivated as possible because it is a big game, but again on big stages you need to take part and have an impact on the game. I've played in big games before and sometimes you think to yourself afterwards "did I actually take part in that game?" but in the Italy game we all took part, we weren't frightened by the stage and we thoroughly deserved the win.'

Italy at home was followed by two games against Azerbaijan when a tie in Belgrade was rescheduled after the Serbian prime minister was assassinated. This rejig proved a blessing in disguise, because after a good start Wales had a chance to keep up their momentum. The support the team was receiving from fans was sky high after the Italy win and they would have fancied their chance against the Azerbaijanis. Wales won both games, despite carrying a number of injuries at the time, and fans started to believe that Wales would reach Portugal and play in Euro 2004.

Finding themselves at the top of their group, the squad's confidence was high. 'When we were top after four games I went to Portugal to pick the hotel,' says Tony Quaglia, 'a Marriott in Lisbon on the coast. So that's how confident we were that we were going to qualify, even though we hadn't even done the hard part and got the job done.' It seems incredible that Wales did that halfway through the group. If Wales had been six games in and still top then it would be understandable. But halfway through qualifying, with away fixtures against the top two seeds in their next two games, where any momentum Wales had already amassed could just be destroyed instantly, it seemed complacent. Matty Jones puts the side's impending collapse down to inexperience. 'You go into every tournament with confidence and belief,' he explains. 'We had such a good start, but it was always going to tail off at the end, because we put so much into the first 45 minutes of every game in a way. International football is a lot more tactical, we lost a lot of games or dropped points right at the death because we've taken our eye off the ball, we got tired, our concentration went, and I'd purely put it down to those factors.'

Wales' collapse started with the rescheduled Serbia game in August, an incredibly awkward time to play an international fixture of such magnitude. There was also a growing sense among those in the media that teams were beginning to work out Wales' game. Whether or not Wales were playing it safe after such a good start, whether it was complacency or whether Wales were just too negative, this is the game where many people thought the campaign fell apart for Wales, as they lost 1–0.

Gary Pritchard, part of the production team for S4C's *Sgorio*, the Welsh equivalent of *Match of the Day*, was in Serbia and recalls his feelings about the game. 'We beat Azerbaijan twice, which was expected,' he says, 'but after that we fell apart as teams really began to figure out Sparky's tactics. The fans were crying out, in the away game against Serbia, for Rob Earnshaw to come on. He was warming up for what felt like ages and, when he'd eventually got on the pitch, he had one shot that was saved. We should have got him on sooner, but that was the game, for me, where it all fell apart.'

If there was to be any hope of restoring the positive momentum that Wales had built in the early part of the campaign, then Hughes' men were going to need to get a result at the San Siro against Italy but, as Jason Koumas acknowledges, Wales were absolutely decimated in Milan. 'The Italy game in the San Siro is something I will never ever forget,' says Koumas. 'They really showed what they were about in that game, especially in the second half where we just could not get near them. They were untouchable. We had a good first half, organised, created a few chances, but just couldn't tuck any of them away. Giggsy had a couple of great chances. Second half they just had too much for us.' To say Italy showed what they were about in that game was a bit of an understatement, as an 11-minute second-half hat-trick for Pipo Inzaghi, as well as a penalty from Alessandro Del Piero with 15 minutes to go, saw Italy annihilate Wales.

After such a heavy defeat the great start to the campaign had almost totally been forgotten. The 4–0 defeat by Italy came almost a year after the opening qualifying game against Finland, and it had been longer still since Wales' positive pre-campaign results, so it is understandable that some, if not all, of that momentum would have been lost after two very damaging defeats. The play-off berth still looked relatively safe at that point, but there wasn't the same atmosphere about the remaining two qualification games as there had been surrounding the previous six; they almost felt like warm-up games for Wales' eventual play-off run. The sad thing is that Wales could have been top of the group, even after that Italy defeat, because if Wales had won their remaining two games – both at home – against Finland and Serbia, then they would have qualified ahead of Italy, but late goals in both games killed their chances of finishing top. Alas, hindsight is a wonderful thing, of course, but Wales' collapse in the second half of the group meant they were now exposed to the ruthlessness of the play-off draw.

A couple of the top-seeded teams found their way into the play-offs, such as Spain and Turkey, but Holland and Russia were also there, as well as Croatia, Norway, Scotland and Slovenia. All of these teams were seeded higher than Wales. Only Latvia were seeded lower and Sod's Law decreed that Wales weren't going to draw them. In the end they drew Russia, which was about as reasonable a draw as Wales could have hoped for, with the added advantage of the second leg being played in Cardiff. So if Wales made a mistake in the first leg they could at least count on 72,000 frantic fans screaming support their way in the return fixture. Wales had to do without two of their best players from the campaign, with Craig Bellamy and Simon Davies missing both games due to injury – absentees that would prove exceptionally costly. Despite this, Wales got their act together for the first leg out in Moscow as they performed excellently to come away with a 0–0 draw. There was no away goal to give added momentum ahead of the return leg but, still, after their previous run of one point in four games, Wales were rightly happy with their performance in the Russian capital. Currently Wales' second-choice goalkeeper, Owain Fôn Williams was only a 16-year-old supporter at the time, but he recalls his feelings towards the play-offs. 'Confidence wasn't that high at the time because of the last few games of that group, but we fancied our chances and thought we might have enough,' he says. 'In the first leg we just couldn't take the lead and that is obviously a big problem. If we could've got a lead for the second leg, then we'd at least have had something to hold onto in that game and perhaps even just played the counterattack, but that wasn't the case and I think it affected us.'

After a very impressive performance away from home in the first leg, Wales struggled under the pressure in the second leg as they didn't really capitalise on the home advantage and never really took the game by the scruff of the neck like they would have been expected to do. Inevitably, Wales' lack of ability to take control of the game resulted in them falling behind early-on as Vadim Evseev headed in a Rolan Gusev free kick. Wales had their chances to equalise, of course, but couldn't take them, as Russia were far too smart and far too tactically aware to give Wales too many good chances and Hughes' team went out of the tournament with a whimper. The absence of Bellamy and Davies in these games was a particular blow, as Wales were quite pedestrian in the second leg and these were two players who could have picked up the pace for Wales and forced the issue a bit more. All in all, Wales just weren't good enough.

After the collapse they'd suffered from the start of the group, did Wales really deserve to qualify? Jason Koumas thinks not. 'In any home game over two legs you have to score and we just couldn't do it,' he says. 'It was so tough. We didn't create anything in the second leg, not for the lack of trying, but I don't think we had enough to break these teams down. It was a great squad with brilliant spirit, but we just didn't have the pace that is crucial in the tight games to enable us to counterattack and put other teams on the back foot.'

There was more controversy to come, as one of the Russian players tested positive for Bromantane, an illegal substance used to enhance athletic performance. The FAW appealed to have action taken against Russia, but it never came to fruition – something Andy Melville was particularly frustrated about. 'I think we were definitely hard done by,' says the Swansea-born defender. 'We told the FAW to take it up and they did, to a certain level, but then the process just stopped for whatever reason, whether it was financial or something else I don't know. If that happened now, I'm not sure if it would have been the same outcome, really, so there's always going to be a massive question mark over that.'

Either way, Wales didn't progress to Portugal. And their collapse from group leaders to losing the play-offs may have been a blessing in disguise. There is a real belief among fans that the Wales team that has qualified for Euro '16 could do something special in the tournament. Could Wales have done it back in 2004 if they'd got there? Maybe not. But then again no-one fancied Greece either back in Euro 2004 and they won the tournament.

Some Wales fans were optimistic, though, because Wales had performed incredibly well when the momentum was on their side. Once they lost it they struggled badly, but that was a lesson many believed Wales would learn from, and the feeling among some supporters was that another campaign under Hughes would lead to success. After all, he was a young manager in his first job. He had been thrown into the deep end and had performed very well on the whole, given the infrastructure he had also started to put in place.

So there were two different trains of thought – those who thought that it was an incredibly positive campaign, and those who thought it was a fantastic opportunity missed. Most wanted Hughes to stay, not least the players. As it turned out, not long afterwards Mark Hughes left the Wales set-up for a job in the Premier League with Blackburn Rovers, so no-one knows what would have happened if he had decided to stick with Wales. Koumas was very happy to play under Hughes. 'I thought he did really well,' says the midfielder. 'It speaks volumes that he went straight into the Premier League afterwards. It was his first job, but you ask any of the players, Giggs, Savage and all of them will back that up. He built the group on spirit, and he was a real influence on me, a top-class guy.'

Around this time Gary Speed was linked with the Wales job for the first time. Speed knew Mark Hughes well, having played with him previously and under him as manager, but it never came about, as Tony Quaglia explains: 'I did tell Speed, at the time Sparky left, to go for the job, but his response was "Quags, they know where I am." I told him it didn't work like that and he just said they knew where he was, which was a shame because Gary should have been the one to succeed Mark.'

Obviously Speed got the job eventually and did continue in the same vein as Hughes, but first came John Toshack in his second stint after an incredibly brief tenure in the mid-1990s. Toshack faced an uphill battle from the start, as a number of senior figures in the side retired, including key squad members Gary Speed, Mark Pembridge and Andy Melville. Some in the media speculated that many senior players retired as a result of Toshack's recent role as a pundit, in which he had criticised the Wales team for their performances. To be fair, as we've seen here briefly, he wasn't the only one criticising Wales, but there was a quite public fallout with midfielder Robbie Savage. Savage told BBC Sport he retired from international football just under a year after Toshack took over because he 'didn't want to be humiliated by being left out of the squad. I think I'm worth more than that.' Savage also commented that Toshack made his decision for him: 'From day one I knew there was a clash of personalities and I think he's cut his nose off to spite his face. He's telling me I'm not good enough to get into a 24-man Wales squad. I'm retiring before he can humiliate me some more.'

The fact that so many players left at the start of Toshack's reign enabled him to bring in the next generation, which of course played a crucial part in where the Wales team finds itself today. With his rugged stance towards the players who decided to leave the set-up, Toshack showed that he was willing to start over. Eleven of the 13 players who would play in the key Euro '16 qualifier against Belgium in Cardiff in June 2015 were given their debuts by him. Toshack could have convinced some of the older heads to stay on, perhaps bringing a few better results with them, but he was willing to sacrifice any short-term gains in order to start the changing of the guard. It would be a fair assessment to say Toshack, and his assistant Brian Flynn, laid the foundations for the future. There were so many talented youngsters available to be brought through. Toshack knew these youngsters weren't going to be ready for their first campaign, or even in two campaigns' time, and that it might take a lot longer. However long it took, he rightly believed that fielding these players at a young age would help them develop into top-class international players. Wales lost a lot of fans during Toshack's reign because they weren't willing to play the waiting game, to see the new kids on the block – the ones whose names the fans now chant so feverishly – learn their craft and gain the experience they needed to become the stars they are today. But Toshack's vision ultimately paid dividends.

One of Toshack's smartest moves was to bring in Brian Flynn to manage the intermediate teams and bring through youth players, the youth players lining up in the starting XI today. The arrangement was different to most international youth set-ups, because Flynn would advise Toshack to promote whoever was ready to the first team rather than ensure each player progressed from level to level until they got to the seniors. This resulted in the likes of Gareth Bale, Joe Ledley and Wayne Hennessey getting their debuts at 16, 17 years old. Flynn was in the ideal position to know about these young talents and bring them through. As his father was heavily involved with the Welsh FA Schools' Association at the time – the Welsh Football Trust did not take charge of most of the younger age groups until 2008 – Flynn would have had more knowledge of those players than most.

There was great excitement about these Welsh youngsters. Although it was accepted they probably weren't going to be ready for a while, their potential was a huge positive. Flynn's impact on some of these players' careers is striking to the point that in researching this book I've been asked by a number of players – Sam Vokes, Jonny Williams and others – to ensure that his contribution to their careers and their development is acknowledged in some way. Flynn wasn't available to speak for the project, which is a shame because for someone who had such an impact on so many careers it would have been great for people to hear his views, but the endorsement of his credentials by so many people speaks for itself.

But despite the undoubted promise of these young players, in reality Toshack struggled to get a consistent team on the pitch for one reason or another. Players pulled out with injuries, legitimate or not. A squad for one international window would quite possibly be totally different to the squad for the next couple of international windows – how could anyone work with that? That said, Wales did get some great results under Toshack. Drawing 0–0 in Germany in Euro 2008 qualifying was one; beating Slovakia 5–2 away was another.

Toshack's tenure tends to get a poor press nowadays, and BBC Wales' football correspondent Rob Phillips believes he was underrated. 'If you look at the clubs he's been to, he is in the highest echelon of British managers,' says Phillips. 'He led Swansea on that meteoric rise they had through the divisions in the '80s where they went from the fourth division to the first in four seasons and he's managed Real Madrid twice. They don't hire mugs as managers in Real. Nobody should underrate his impact, he was maligned at the time, maybe because he never had a marquee win. Sparky had one against Italy, Terry Yorath had Germany, Tosh didn't have any of those.' On top of that, Toshack has the second highest win percentage of any Wales manager, bettered only by Gary Speed who won half of his games compared to Toshack who won 42 per cent of his.

Despite the positives, it was going to take an awful lot for Toshack to be able to stay in charge for as long as was needed to see these players realise their potential – something they've only consistently started to do much more recently. Some thought the Euro 2012 qualifying campaign was the one where Wales might be in with a chance of returning to some form of glory, but defeat in the opening game against Montenegro got everything off to a bad start and Toshack resigned soon afterwards, saying he hoped that his decision to leave the post early in qualifying would help keep Wales' qualification hopes alive.

Jack Collison, one of many of the current crop given his debut by Toshack, is full of praise for his former manager. 'I've said it before that the chances we all had to play in the senior squads as youngsters was massive for our development,' says Collison. 'You look through the squad now, Gunter, Ramsey, Bale, they've got so many caps at such a young age and are so experienced, and still have so much more football to play, so you can't disregard what Toshack did by giving the youngsters a chance at such a young age. Unfortunately he suffered the poor results and the sometimes below-par performances from the team, but the likes of Gary Speed and Chris Coleman afterwards have really reaped the rewards.'

FAW chief executive Jonathan Ford, who worked with Toshack for a brief period of time after taking over as CEO of the FAW in the 2009/10 season, is also full of praise for the former Real Madrid boss. 'I've got an awful lot of respect for John,' he says. 'The job that most people really would rate him on is bringing the squad from an old generation of players that we had at the time that he came in, following that Euro 2004 qualifying campaign. John's job was to make those big changes happen and bring through a younger element. A lot of people would turn around and say that appointing Brian Flynn, identifying a lot of key young players, a lot of the good work we're seeing now, the foundation stones were laid by John Toshack. Did John have his time? He resigned, we didn't get rid of him, he turned around and said he thought he had taken the team as far as he could and we respected that.'

With Toshack gone, Brian Flynn stepped in to take temporary charge of the side. However Flynn's two games in charge resulted in two defeats to Bulgaria and Switzerland, so he soon had some very healthy competition to deal with when it came to finding a full-time successor to develop the work he and Toshack had done.

PART 2

'Unveiling Gary Speed opened a
new chapter for football in our country'

STEVE WILLIAMS

CHAPTER 3

The benchmark for a nation:
Wales' most-lauded, most-loved footballer

'Very few international footballers can be compared to Gary
Speed. How many footballers have played for, captained and
managed their country with the same distinction?'

DON MURRAY, WALES FAN

THERE CAN BE no mistaking Gary Speed's significance to
Welsh football. Wales have seldom had a player so consistent,
a player who has seemed to be involved in so many of the
country's most crucial footballing moments. It was Speed
who won *that* penalty against Romania when he was fouled
by Dan Petrescu, and he was a big part of that whole 1994
qualifying campaign. Andy Williams' classic song 'Can't Take
My Eyes Off You', which was used by BBC Wales in a promo
video for that campaign became Wales fans' anthem of
choice for the midfielder – a song that was later re-recorded
by Kelly Jones of the Stereophonics in tribute to Speed's
memory. Speed scored the winning goal against Moldova
in 1995 that broke a six-game winless streak in Euro '96
qualifying, was heavily involved in the resurgence under
Mark Hughes and was brilliant when he took his talents to
the touchline for Wales in 2011. In every game he would
give the absolute maximum for his team, always leaving
everything on the pitch, always leading the way. If you were
to ask Welsh fans to rank the country's players, captains
and managers in terms of significance, Gary Speed's legacy
would be obvious.

Very few people in international football compare to Gary Speed. When you put everything into perspective, only the likes of Franz Beckenbauer, Jürgen Klinsmann and Michel Platini compare to the Welshman in all-round international footballing terms. How many other footballers have given as much to their country's football team as a player, captain and manager? Very few people in international football have accomplished all three of those feats, fewer still have done it with the grace, integrity and passion shown by those four.

Gary Speed played 85 times, 44 times as captain, for a small nation of three million people which had rarely done anything significant at the top level of international football before, but in every stage of his international career his presence gave the country hope that one day, under his leadership, whether that be on the pitch or from the touchline, Wales' fortunes might change. When he came in to manage the side after the Toshack era, we eventually saw some of the best football Wales has ever played, with Speed attaining the best win percentage of any Wales manager in history. As a footballer, as an athlete, as a person, as an all-round human being he was elite, absolutely top-drawer, and he will forever be remembered as such by everyone who ever came across him.

Former teammates, opponents, coaches, managers, supporters, journalists – whoever I talked to about Gary Speed during the research for this book reacted in the same way. In every interview, adoration. Every time his name was mentioned, fond words and cherished memories followed. Even now that he's left us, Gary Speed can still light up a room. I've never experienced anything like it.

No Welsh football fan will ever forget waking up on that November morning in 2011 and hearing the news; in the internet age you're used to hoaxes and sick things like that and I remember hoping that this was one such hoax. I even texted a friend saying exactly that. I had no basis for thinking that way. I just didn't believe that what I'd heard was in any way possible. The entire football community in Britain was thinking the same, but it wasn't the case. It was real, and no-one could believe it – Gary Speed had left us. So many had watched him on the BBC's *Football Focus* programme the day before. Robbie Savage said he had spoken to him the day before and he had seemed his normal self. There was nothing to suggest anything even remotely like this was going to happen. Bryn Law, Sky Sports News journalist and a good friend of Gary Speed, broke down on air the following evening when recollecting his memories of him. Craig Bellamy was in bits. All of those closest to Gary Speed were torn in half by the tragic news of his passing – Chris Coleman, Osian Roberts, everyone who had ever came into contact with him, not to mention Speed's incredible family. God knows how they coped.

The family say they have received millions of messages of support since Gary Speed's passing and that doesn't surprise me whatsoever. The man was unbelievable – he did everything for everyone. He even ventured to Anglesey, where I live, to appear at a charity event to raise awareness for men's cancer causes. He didn't charge a penny, brought his own memorabilia to sell in the charity auction, spent time chatting to every single person, an exemplary human being. That was ten days before he passed – if you'd have told anyone in that room that ten days later Gary Speed wouldn't be with us, then everyone would have called you mad. It didn't seem in any way possible.

Howard Wilkinson, Speed's first manager in professional football, was one of many people I approached to talk about Speed and he, like everyone, spoke very highly of him. 'Football needs people like him,' says Wilkinson, who took a Leeds United team containing Gary Speed to the First Division title in 1992. 'He was a credit to the game, an example of football's good side. Most important, though, is the effect he had on those who really knew him. When I was told the news early that Sunday morning I was rocked to the core. As time passes, I frequently find myself wondering if I could have done anything. As far as his family, Louise, the boys, his parents and sister, one cannot begin to imagine their pain. They should all feel extremely proud though, in that his success as a person and a player was to a large degree down to what they all gave him.'

Everyone was reeling from his passing and it was touching to see so many people rally behind the family and those closest to Speed at such a desperately difficult time, and how everyone has remembered his work throughout every step of the journey that Welsh football has been on since.

I can't possibly give the most in-depth account of Speed's career as a player. Writers such as Paul Abbandonato have done that elsewhere so much better than I ever could, so what follows is a brief summary of what kind of a man and player he was.

Gary Speed's class and potential as a person and a footballer was obvious long before he pulled on the lilywhite shirt for Leeds United. He was making a huge impression on the footballing community even as a ten year old, because he just had everything. Cledwyn Ashford, Speed's coach as a youngster, summarised how gifted the midfielder was at such a young age. 'He played for Deeside Primary Schools at age nine, ten and 11,' says Ashford. 'He was an exceptional player, even at that young age, very talented. Very bright too, academically and on the pitch. He was our captain, he scored the most goals, made the most appearances and so on – he was a fine, fine player.'

There's a great story from around this time where Ashford's team, which Speed captained, were invited to the Jersey Festival – an enormous football festival for primary school pupils attended by hundreds of people from across the United Kingdom, from kids to parents, teachers, coaches. You'd forgive a young boy like Speed for being intimidated in that environment, especially when it came to thanking the organisers for putting on such an event. The coaches would normally do that, but a ten-year-old Gary Speed had other ideas, as Ashford notes. 'Even at the age of ten and 11, he would speak in front of hundreds of people at the Jersey Festival and thank them all for their welcome,' says Ashford.

'He would take it upon himself as captain to do that without any difficulty whatsoever.'

As he grew up, Speed progressed to the regional under-14s, again playing under Ashford, before he went for a Wales trial at under-15 level. He was turned down. They didn't think he was big or strong enough to compete at international level so he didn't get selected – I wonder where those selectors are now? Speed kept progressing through the regional teams, though, captaining the north Wales side, before going to Leeds where he would be introduced to a group of people and new concepts that were fundamental in enabling him to develop into the midfield maestro that he became.

What convinced Wilkinson to give Speed his debut in the first team back in 1988 wasn't simply the Welshman's talent, 'When I first saw him at the age of about 17/18 he was talented, but so were others,' recalls Wilkinson. 'What I saw in him was more to do with character, honesty, desire and team-mindedness. He played in every position in the team at Leeds apart from in goal for me without any problem. Always gave it his best shot. There's not many people you can say that about. Never a word of complaint, whenever he was in the team he played for the team, never for Gary Speed.' You hear all the time these days of modern players saying they just want to play football and don't care where they play – most of them mean they'll play on the right and the left wing, or play in one position or another – but none of them embody that like Speed did.

Players like Gordon Strachan, Gary McAllister, Chris Fairclough and David Batty were ideal role models for Speed throughout his formative years in top-level football. The latter even informed Speed that Terry Venables wanted him to play for England if he was interested, as Speed was the first Welsh-born member of a predominantly English family, but he refused as he was adamant he wanted to represent Wales.

The second, perhaps most significant aspect of professional football that the Welshman was introduced to at Leeds United was the emerging phenomenon of sports science. A lot of people say Arsène Wenger was the first to bring the emphasis on sports science and nutrition into British football but that's not strictly true. Howard Wilkinson at Leeds was the first, and Speed fully embraced that. Strachan was an enormous influence on the midfielder too, a fitter man than Speed when the young Welshman joined the club despite Strachan being in his early thirties. Speed spent as much time studying the Scot's fitness methods as possible. His willingness to learn and develop understandings of new concepts and ideas was one of the many characteristics that were instrumental in making him the success he became on and off the pitch.

By 1990, Speed had won the Second Division with Leeds, playing 25 league games and scoring three goals in the league campaign as a 20 year old. He was selected by Terry Yorath towards the end of that 89/90 season to make his Wales debut against Costa Rica at Ninian Park in a 1–0 win. Rob Phillips recalls his initial impressions of the midfielder. 'The first time I remember him being involved in a Wales squad was for a game against Holland in Wrexham – he didn't get on the pitch that night. I knew nothing about him, but I was doing a column with Terry Yorath at the time and he was adamant that this unknown quantity was decent. A year later he demonstrated what would soon become an obvious commitment to Wales, as he played in an under-21 game in Merthyr one night, then played against Costa Rica the next. That's when I first saw him. He looked great, so composed on the ball. As I got to know him better I realised he was a really composed character all-round. He was just a really good guy.'

Both Andy Melville and Speed came into the squad at around the same time and Melville recalled how quickly Speed took to international football. 'On and off the pitch he was the perfect professional,' says Melville. 'He always had time for you. We spent a lot of time together. On the pitch he was a leader, [he] set an example every day in training, no negatives about him whatsoever. Wales had ups and downs over the years and in those downs he'd come alive, he'd stand up and be a big character in the changing room. It can be daunting as a young lad to join up with the likes of Ian Rush, Mark Hughes, Neville Southall, but he integrated very well, it didn't faze him at all, he just took it in his stride and never looked back from there.'

Domestically, Speed continued to flourish. In their first season back in the First Division, Leeds finished fourth, before winning the title the following year – for the last time before the Premier League behemoth took over. Speed, still in his early twenties, played 41 of the 42 league games in that title-winning season, playing in a number of positions and scoring seven goals. Nowadays we're used to seeing players accomplishing big feats at such a young age, but back then it wasn't very common. Gary Speed was bucking the trend and British football was noticing.

Many hailed that Leeds midfield of Strachan, Batty, McAllister and Speed as one of the greatest midfields in the modern era. It really had been a remarkable start to the Welshman's professional career, but his manager wasn't surprised. 'He was a quick learner,' says Wilkinson. 'A good listener. Someone who really wanted to get better, who wanted to understand as much as he possibly could about the game, what it took to be successful and what it meant to be professional in all senses of the word. No matter what the circumstances were he always gave 100 per cent. As a young, handsome, successful professional footballer he had his moments, but it only took one serious heart-to-heart to get him back on track. Any manager would have been delighted to have worked with somebody like Gary. He was high performance and low maintenance, a manager's dream.' That Speed was the Leeds fans' dream, too, was demonstrated after his death when they chanted, 'We all dream of a team of Gary Speeds'.

Having learnt a number of lessons through his relationship with Wilkinson and by playing games in the Champions League for Leeds United, Speed had accomplished incredible things at an extremely young age. But Wilkinson was thinking further ahead. 'I remember I sat down with him very early on in his career and told him that he had the makings of being a leader,' remembers Wilkinson. 'He was surprised, even shocked and laughed nervously. He was a little bit embarrassed about it, I think, but I explained to him: "You do things right, you lead by example, you always give your best for the team, your performance really matters. As you get older people will start to be influenced by you and as you recognise this you'll grow and do more and you will start to see it as a responsibility you have for others." He took that on board and as his career progressed he became one of those characters that players need and managers appreciate. I wasn't surprised he became the leader he did, it was always what he was going to do and what he wanted to do.'

Speed's willingness to embrace the leadership role saw him bond with some of the youth players at Leeds, including Matty Jones, who would become a very close friend in the years to come. 'I was 12 years old and Gary acted as my older brother when he took me in at Leeds United,' says Jones, who played 13 times for Wales. 'I was a newcomer and he really supported me. The advice he gave me back then is that none of us are born with natural ability and natural talent. We earn our right. We give 100 per cent, not 90 per cent, not 110 per cent, because there's no such thing. You give your all. He wasn't born a natural at heading, a natural tackler, nor was he born with that fitness, but it was because he worked so hard at it that he was such an all-round player and that's the advice I took from him.'

With such an emphasis on giving 100 per cent at all times, there was only one club Gary Speed could support: Everton. The legend on the club's emblem, *Nil Satis Nisi Optimum* (Nothing But The Best Is Good Enough), are words that Speed embodied and, after amassing 312 appearances and 57 goals for Leeds United, stamping his authority on the game at 26 years old, he completed a dream move by signing for the Merseyside club in 1996, a club he had supported so avidly since he was a boy. Manager Joe Royle reveals why he was 'very, very keen' to bring Speed to Everton. 'I'd always admired him when he was a player at Leeds,' says Royle, a former Toffees striker. 'He was terrific in the air, a great finisher on his left-foot and he worked for the team. It was a great signing for us. I remember speaking with his agent at the time and he told me that Gary had told him to just get the deal done, because of how much he wanted to join Everton, so it was done very quickly.'

Arriving on Merseyside, Speed was approaching his prime as a player. He was living closer to his parents and playing for the club of his dreams. It all seemed perfect, and things started off that way as he scored on his debut at Goodison Park in a 2–0 win over Kevin Keegan's Newcastle United, stealing the limelight from Alan Shearer who was making his debut for his boyhood club after signing from Blackburn Rovers.

A few more good results followed, before Everton's inconsistent season turned disastrous, with the club finishing in a lowly 16th place at the end of the season. The only highlights the fans were treated to came from Speed, who was pretty much unanimously recognised as the club's best player at the time. He'd looked like a man possessed against Southampton in November 1996, as he'd scored his only career hat-trick and got an assist on the way to helping Everton demolish the opposition 7–1. And he scored a great equaliser against Liverpool in front of The Kop at Anfield just four days afterwards.

Royle left the club towards the end of that season, but recalls his pride that the Welshman had been such a success at the club. 'His debut sticks out,' says Royle. 'The equaliser at Anfield, where he did what he did so often in his career and found space with a great leap for the header. We were being talked about as outsiders for the Premier League at that point. It never came to fruition, but Gary was involved in all of our best moments when he was at the club. I'm proud and pleased that he was successful for Everton – it was a shame I wasn't around longer to work with him, because he was a pleasure to work with.'

Speed was unanimously voted Everton's Player of the Year at the end of the season, finishing as the club's joint-top-scorer with 11 goals alongside Duncan Ferguson – an excellent goal return for a midfielder whose primary task wasn't necessarily to finish off plays. It was perhaps an illustration of just how much Everton were struggling that Speed took it upon himself to score so many goals.

At the end of that season, Speed was made Wales captain by Bobby Gould; something Speed called the 'high spot' of his career and his proudest moment at the time. As a decision, Speed's good friend and teammate Iwan Roberts thinks it was a no-brainer. 'I wasn't surprised when he was made Welsh captain at such an early age,' says Roberts. 'He was a leader. You could tell when he spoke in the dressing room that he had captain qualities, he had managerial qualities. You could tell by the way he spoke about the game. A fantastic leader of men, he had the utmost respect of all of his fellow professionals.'

On a personal level, things seemingly got even better for Speed as he was named club captain at Everton by Howard Kendall, who replaced Royle in time for the 1997/98 season. But as good a captain as Speed was, it would take more than that to fix Everton as results went from bad to worse under Kendall, and Speed left the set-up in the next transfer window. Although he'd been there for less than two seasons, Speed's impact at Everton was plain for all to see. The fact that he was jeered so much when he returned to play against Everton for Newcastle United showed how special a player the fans thought they were losing.

In retrospect, there aren't many players that Everton have sold since then that have left more of a hole in the side than he did, nor have they signed anyone anywhere near his class. Neville Southall, as well as playing a number of games with Speed for Wales, played with him at Everton during that period and summarised his experience of the midfielder. 'As a person I don't think you could get any better,' says Southall, who made 578 appearances for Everton as well as 92 for Wales. 'He was a proper footballer and a proper geezer. He was the right kind of stubborn. He always gave his all to the team and if you're the captain you do take on more responsibility and he was excellent at that. He was always out on his own before training, getting ready, and I thought he brought that professionalism into every club he went to, especially at Everton. Personally, I think he left Everton because he wanted pasta and not fish and chips on the bus, and that's the kind of guy he was. Maybe he didn't think Everton were as professional as they should be and, I have to say, when I was there with him at that time, I'd probably agree with him.'

Kenny Dalglish signed Speed for Newcastle United for £5.5m in February 1998, a move that has since been hailed as Dalglish's best signing for the club during his tenure. Goalkeeper Shay Given, another great signing by the Scot, had only joined The Toon six months previously but was relieved to see Speed join the club. 'He was a fantastic midfielder and he brought a real presence with him,' says Given. 'He fitted in really well and really quickly. His personality, his confidence and his belief in himself rubbed off on everyone at the club. He was a real infectious guy, people wanted to be around him, he was jovial and a great guy to be around. He was a machine fitness-wise, a real freak, ripped, box-to-box and great in the air, so it was nice to have him on my team rather than against me!' Given had encountered Speed for the first time six months earlier, when Everton travelled to Newcastle for a Premier League fixture, and the experience had surprised the goalkeeper. 'We were just in the tunnel and he was like "Alright Shay?" which took me back a little because I was still young then. I felt important because he said hello to me.'

Despite taking Newcastle to an FA Cup final at the end of the 1997/98 season, where United were beaten 2–0 by that season's league winners Arsenal, Dalglish was sacked two games into the following season and replaced by Sir Bobby Robson. Sir Bobby's admiration for Speed was obvious, no more so than when Speed left the club and Robson told Sky Sports, 'I could stand here for another ten minutes and talk about Gary Speed, I just want to give him the accolade that he deserves. He'll be missed, he'll be missed in the dressing rooms, in the training rooms, restaurants, planes, buses; in every concept that boy was involved when he came in to play for Newcastle United, he will be missed.' To Shay Given it was 'obvious' that manager and player enjoyed a real closeness, despite the fact that neither wanted to show it often in front of the other players.

Speed's impact on Newcastle was enormous. In the six years that he played for the club, some excellent players would grace the St James' Park pitch: Alan Shearer, Craig Bellamy, Nolberto Solano, Rob Lee, David Batty, to name just a few. But, to Robson's assistant manager John Carver, Speed was the glue that held the team together. 'Gary was the key to that team because of his experience, his leadership qualities,' says Carver. 'Everybody had so much respect for him, all the young lads, Jermaine Jenas, Kieron Dyer, Aaron Hughes, Olivier Bernard, they all looked up to Gary and his experience helped those younger players develop.' Some have said that this was the strongest Newcastle side in the club's history, so to say Speed was such a huge part of that speaks volumes for the Welshman's quality. After a difficult last few months at Everton, Speed had seemed reinvigorated at the heart of the Newcastle midfield, and claimed later in his career that his time in the north-east was the happiest in his playing career. Not shackled with defensive responsibilities, Speed was given the freedom to express himself and get forward as much as possible, chipping in with some very important goals along the way both domestically and in Europe, as Newcastle featured in the Champions League in the 2002/03 season.

While Newcastle were putting in some strong seasons in the Premier League, challenging the top four regularly during Speed's time at the club, Wales under Mark Hughes were flourishing, too, and the part Speed played in that cannot be understated. Obviously, being Hughes' captain he had a huge influence, but his professionalism, leadership, the way he helped the youngsters greatly aided Hughes to extract the best out of what was a good, balanced Wales team. Speed's impact on Craig Bellamy, one of Wales' brightest sparks, shouldn't be overlooked either. He was always giving the striker advice, looking out for him, getting the best out of him. Bellamy says as much himself in his autobiography, *Goodfellas*. Kit Symons was a very close friend of Speed's, having played with him since the two were together in the Wales under-17s, and he felt the midfielder was pivotal to Wales' performances under Hughes: 'He was very influential,' says Symons. 'He was always an important part of the team throughout his Welsh career, but during that spell where he was captain he was instrumental to the success of the side. We had some fantastic performances along the way and some real good times – Gary was pivotal to all of that.'

Jason Koumas, another of Wales' youth prospects during the Hughes era, roomed with Speed while on Wales duty and can't speak highly enough of his teammate. 'He got the lads going,' says Koumas. 'He was probably the best player in our team for God knows how many years. I doubt anyone has told you differently but as a person, Speed was a class fella, always giving advice, great to play alongside. You could tell he was going to be a great manager; on the pitch he just spoke to everyone, treated everyone the same and was a natural leader. I feel privileged to have known him.'

Unfortunately for Speed, Wales didn't qualify for Euro 2004 after their qualification push was stopped in its tracks at the last hurdle against Russia, but his impact on the team and how much he brought to the table at that time, and throughout his career, was never in doubt. What was unclear was his future at Newcastle, as Speed wasn't offered a new contract by the club, despite desperate attempts by Sir Bobby Robson to convince the board to give one of his key players the contract he felt he deserved. So Speed left the club after six very satisfying years. John Carver was surprised at the board's stubbornness. 'He wanted to stay, I wanted him to stay, Sir Bobby wanted him to stay, the players wanted him to stay,' says Carver. 'I don't think Gary realised at the time that it was nothing to do with Sir Bobby, it was a decision made at board level and it was taken out of Bobby's hands. Gary was very disappointed when he had to leave, he didn't want to leave, his home was here and his family loved it here, this was his home.'

At 34, and on the verge of leaving a club at which he'd been an icon for so long, you could forgive a player who had been as dynamic and had as much of an impact as Speed had managed to have throughout his career for deciding to hang his boots up and call it a day. He was never going to do that, though, was he? Having played over 50 games the previous season for Newcastle United, there was no doubting how fit he was. The fire was still burning strongly, and a move to Bolton Wanderers beckoned, where he would form some relationships that would prove key going into the remainder of his playing career and his time as a manager.

A number of his former clubs were very keen to take Gary Speed back, such was the impact that everyone saw Speed would still have on a team, as Sam Allardyce recalls when he signed the Welshman for Bolton. 'David Moyes was ringing him and pestering him every 15 minutes on the phone,' says Allardyce. 'I told him to answer it and speak to him, because if he wanted to go to Everton then he should go. He answered the phone to David and politely told him that he was at Bolton with me, that he wanted to sign for me, that he wasn't going to change his mind and there was no need to keep ringing, and that doesn't happen very often – believe you me.'

You could understand another man perhaps playing Everton and Bolton off against each other in order to get a better deal, but not Gary Speed. Incredibly, though, Allardyce also notes how his chairman needed convincing of Speed's quality. 'The chairman at the time didn't want to sign him because of his age,' recalls Allardyce. 'But the easy thing for me was that we had Gary's Pro-zone stats. They showed his level of performance on the field, which matched a 25 year old's still, so we quickly shut the chairman up by showing him Gary's stats from the last season at Newcastle. We could show that he was going to be one of the best players that Bolton had had. It was never about money with Gary, all he wanted to do was play.'

Speed went on to stand out in a very good squad at Bolton, a squad including Jay-Jay Okocha, Kevin Nolan, Kevin Davies, Fernando Hierro, Ivan Campo and others. The success the team had during his stay was astounding, achieving a level of consistency that would only be bettered by clubs with significantly bigger budgets and significantly more star power than Bolton. It was a real testament to the work Allardyce and his team were doing at Bolton at the time. Speed's relationship with his manager would be key later on in the Welshman's career as he would regularly seek managerial tips from Allardyce. But a meeting with sports science guru Damian Roden on his first day at Bolton would lead to another relationship pivotal to Speed's future success. 'I had to do a fitness test on him,' remembers Roden. 'Being a proud Welshman and a fan of the Welsh national team I was in awe of him, as you can imagine. I was amazed how down to earth he was, very professional in everything he did, but as a person it was just like sitting there and talking to a friend. I was ecstatic, he was one of my role models, one of my idols being the Welsh captain. I was immensely excited because I was going to be working with him on a daily basis. From day one, I'd go out early to set-up the sessions and the warm-ups and he'd already be out there getting himself ready and we just sort of formed a relationship from there really.'

It says much about Speed that after all he had achieved in the game and given how highly regarded he was, he was still putting in the effort to find any extra edge. Bolton was the perfect place for him to flourish physically, as Allardyce had very much expanded on the principles first introduced to Speed by Howard Wilkinson and Gordan Strachan at Leeds United. Allardyce brought in technology to complement a thorough nutritional and physical regime that Speed had already adopted himself, and introduced sports psychologists and a host of other innovative concepts. Such was the effectiveness of the club's approach to player wellbeing that those who knew Speed said the work the Welshman did with Allardyce, Roden and the sports science infrastructure at Bolton extended his career by a good few years.

The midfielder's incredible international career, however, was about to come to an end, after Wales lost 3-2 to Poland in a World Cup qualifier in Cardiff. Speaking to the BBC, Speed said he felt it was the right time to make the decision. 'I'm finished,' he said. 'That's me. The time is right. It looks difficult for us to qualify now and it would be wrong for me to carry on. It's time to get someone younger in for the next campaign. I have had a great career and loved every minute.'

Having become Wales' most-capped outfield player with 85 caps – including a record 44 caps as captain – and given his incredible fitness, Speed could have quite easily hunted down Neville Southall's overall record of 92 caps for his country and become Wales' all-time most-capped player. But showing the kind of integrity and modesty that football fans loved him for, he said he wouldn't do it, because he didn't want to insult Southall by simply carrying on to beat his record. There were calls from his former international teammates to step into the void Mark Hughes had left with Wales and manage the side going forward, but it would take a few more years for that to come to fruition.

There were more incredible achievements to follow for Speed at the Reebok, as Speed was able to now use international breaks to recuperate, getting his body into as good a shape as possible for the latter stages of his career. On the day that Chelsea won their first league title for 50 years, with Jose Mourinho's side beating Allardyce's side 2–0 at the Reebok, the Welshman achieved the unbelievable landmark of 700 club matches. It was an amazing achievement, unfortunately overshadowed by Chelsea's title win, that served as the icing on the cake for Speed's fantastic first season at Bolton. Speed turned out in more than 40 games as Bolton impressed many achieving a club-record sixth-place finish in the Premier League, securing a UEFA Cup berth for the 2005/06 season. Another 40-game haul followed the following season as Bolton continued to impress. They might not have reached the same heights domestically as the previous season but, with European football to contend with, as well as the rigorous domestic schedule of English football, that was perhaps to be expected.

On a personal level the records continued to tumble as, in December 2006, Speed became the first player to notch up 500 Premier League appearances. Naturally, the tributes flooded in from all over football. His captain, his manager, opposition managers, the tabloids were all full of praise for this ever-present, dynamic midfielder who was now much closer to 40 than 30.

However the good times soon became harder to find at Bolton, as Allardyce took the surprise decision to leave the club in April 2007. He later cited the club's lack of ambition to reach for the heights he felt they could achieve, by not spending the money required to break into the top four, as his reason for leaving the post after eight years at the helm.

Sammy Lee came in to replace him for the coming season and Speed was given a role as a player-coach. It was the first step on the coaching ladder for Speed, but it didn't last long as Lee 'relieved' Speed of his coaching duties, deciding he wanted him to 'focus on his game'. Speed contradicted this, saying he had made the decision to step down. The existence of tension between Lee and his players was further evidenced by the fact that Speed and club captain Kevin Nolan found themselves benched for a big game against Chelsea, and the new manager was sacked less than three months into the new season.

Gary Megson became the club's third manager in just over six months. The lack of stability at the club was a nightmare for any player, but it was more so for Speed who had found himself pushed from pillar to post. A player under Allardyce, he had become a player-coach under Lee, before being benched and then thrust back into the starting line-up under Megson. After such a successful spell under Allardyce, through no fault of Speed's, the club had found itself in quite a mess.

Under Megson, Speed featured rarely for Bolton and soon took the decision to move on to play for Bryan Robson, manager at Sheffield United in the Championship. The move marked the end of his Premier League career, during which he had amassed 535 appearances and 80 goals, scoring in each season of the Premier League that he featured in, an incredible 16 seasons on the trot. It was a record only bettered by Ryan Giggs, Paul Scholes and Frank Lampard. Signing for Sheffield United and making his debut on the same day, New Year's Day 2008, Speed was a key target for Robson. The former Manchester United and England captain had tried to acquire him from Bolton over the summer but had been turned away. Club chairman Terry Robinson praised Speed's experience as a key factor in wanting to sign him, with the hope that he could drive the Blades on to a promotion push.

As it turned out, Robson would not stay in the job long enough to be able to work extensively with the player he'd chased so insistently. The side suffered a bad run of results and he was replaced by Kevin Blackwell. Blackwell made Speed the hub of his team and United went on to win eight and draw one of their last 11 games. The following season saw Sheffield United earn a place in the play-offs, but the club missed out on promotion. Speed had played 17 league games as the Blades found themselves fourth by November, but he came off after ten minutes against Wolves with an injury. It was a collector's item for Speed to come off at all, never mind after ten minutes, with a problem. Everything pointed to this injury being something serious and so it proved, as his back injury was deemed serious enough to require surgery. Speed initially painted an optimistic picture, hoping to be back in the fold before the end of the season to aid the club in what he was adamant – and was later proved right – would be a promotion push, but his return never materialised.

In his absence from the pitch, Speed was able to take some time to get acquainted with the side of the game that everyone knew he was going to go into when he hung up his boots. He became so engrossed with coaching that he admitted to not missing playing too much as a result. Speed spent the entire 2009/10 season developing his coaching skills with Blackwell and his assistant Sam Ellis, before calling time on an incredible playing career in May 2010. He then signed a one-year deal to stay on as part of the club's coaching team on a permanent basis. Other clubs, such as Swansea City, were aware of the Welshman's potential as a coach and made enquiries about his availability. But all approaches were rebuffed, a hint to Sheffield United's long-term plans for Speed. Sure enough, three games into the 2010/11 season, after a bad start, Blackwell was sacked and Speed was promoted to the hot seat.

Three months into Speed's reign, with a distinct style of play being developed and points won from half of their matches, things had improved for Sheffield United. But before anyone could really see what he could do with a full season at the club under his belt, his country came calling, and we all know what happened next.

CHAPTER 4

Shifting the foundations of the Welsh game – Gary Speed's managerial tenure

'You always thought you had a chance with Gary Speed in charge, because he was a winner, very much so, and that rubbed off on everyone else around him'

CHRIS WHITLEY, CHAIRMAN, FAW INTERNATIONAL BOARD

WHEN THE FOOTBALL Association of Wales' CEO Jonathan Ford was appointed to the role in December 2009, his remit for the job was very much a modernisation quest, in the sense that some of the FAW's processes were in need of updating. The work Ford wanted to do was comprehensive. He saw the need to change many things. The manager wasn't one of them, as Ford was happy with John Toshack. But once he had a vacancy to fill it was the perfect opportunity to continue that modernisation process in footballing terms too, not just commercially, with a manager who fitted that bill, who wanted to further modernise the set-up. Any potential candidate for the job would have to enhance and modernise Welsh football in every sense. Not just internationals, but also the domestic league and the youth development aspect. They had to identify areas of the infrastructure that needed improvement and know how to go about doing it. Basically they needed an all-encompassing vision for improving the profile and the status of the game and its future in Wales.

As with any high-profile job in football, you don't need to advertise it because the media do that for you. Toshack had unearthed and assembled a squad with so much potential that many were keen to be considered for the job. After going through due diligence, vetting CVs, whittling down the candidates and fitting all those remaining into the Association's recruitment profile, the FAW chose seven candidates to interview: Brian Flynn, Dean Saunders, John Hartson, Lawrie Sanchez, Lars Lagerbäck, Chris Coleman and Gary Speed. It was an eclectic mix of managerial talent, and it speaks for the calibre of the Welsh team at the time that someone like Lagerbäck was interested in the job, given what he had done previously with Sweden and has done since with Iceland, leading them to qualification for Euro 2016. In terms of managerial experience, it looked unlikely that Speed would get the job. Compared to the likes of Coleman, Sanchez and Lagerbäck, he didn't have much, but it was all about fitting a profile, not fulfilling one specific criterion. For Steve Williams, a FAW councillor who was on the FAW's selection panel, Speed had experience in other areas that his rival candidates couldn't match. 'Gary was inexperienced,' says Williams, 'but he had more experience than Mark Hughes did when he got the job. Mark went straight from playing to managing Wales, whereas Gary had sixth months managing Sheffield United, so there's two sides to it. How much more experience of our set-up could you look for though than a guy who played for Wales 85 times, 44 times as captain? He had so much experience of international football, working with people, liaising with a manager as a captain – there were a lot of attributes there that gave me a heart-warming feeling about his candidacy.'

In order to narrow down their shortlist to a more manageable two or three potential options, the FAW asked each candidate the same set of questions, with each answer being scored out of ten. The conversation would then become about how each individual fitted what the FAW was looking for, and which man fitted it best. Gary Speed was awarded the position, ahead of his eventual successor Chris Coleman – both very marketable individuals who improved the profile of the FAW.

'We certainly needed to improve the profile of the FAW,' explains Ford, 'and Gary was young, dynamic and had a clear vision for the game. You could take Gary anywhere and he would instantly fit in. When he came on board, we had a staff football team that he was a part of; the staff went out on payday pub trips and Gary would go out with them; when we did collections for birthdays or whatever he would make sure he donated. He was a shining light who came into the office beaming with smiles. The sun shone when he was around.'

A clear indication of how much the FAW wanted Speed to take the job of manager was the significant compensation fee paid to Sheffield United to release him. Trefor Lloyd Hughes, who was FAW vice-president at the time, saw Speed's vision for the game in Wales as a huge factor in his appointment. 'He brought a different type of vision to what we had seen previously in the role and he was exceptionally keen to push that vision,' he says. 'Gary showed us his enthusiasm. He wanted to develop a "Welsh Way". His knowledge and his understanding of people was crucial as well. He was very professional, keen, enthusiastic and he wanted to show people that there was a different way of thinking about the game in Wales, especially at international level.'

Lagerbäck had been the media's favourite candidate, with one journalist in particular that I spoke to hailing his potential appointment as 'a revolutionary appointment by the FAW at a time when it needed radical change'. Little did this journalist know that Speed would turn out to be just as revolutionary. Rob Phillips admits that he was also surprised that Lagerbäck wasn't chosen. 'It was a big gamble that they went for Gary Speed,' says Phillips. 'I must admit, I thought Lagerbäck would've been a good manager of Wales. He's shown that he's good at turning teams into solid contenders. But you have to say looking back that picking Speed was an inspired choice.'

Gary Speed's appointment as manager was seen as the opening of a new chapter for football in Wales. But why? What did he do? Well, the first thing any new manager has to do is bring in their backroom staff and Gary Speed made some astute choices. Osian Roberts, technical director of the Welsh Football Trust, was brought in to join the senior team, having taken Speed through his coaching badges. Roberts is very well-regarded in world football for his knowledge and tactical understanding and was key to Speed's vision in terms of how the youth development process was streamlined. He also planned and implemented the many infrastructure changes – bringing in sports scientists, match evaluation methods, etc. – that Speed deemed essential. Roberts' influence on and immense understanding of the intricacies of Welsh football is clear to see. His skillset was the perfect complement to Speed's. While the manager knew the playing set-up like the back of his hand, having been involved with it longer than most in his playing days, Roberts was among the most knowledgeable in terms of the coaching and tactical side of the Welsh game.

Of course, being the embodiment of longevity throughout his playing career, Gary Speed was always going to want the best in terms of coaches with a background in fitness and sports science for his team. Sticking with what he knew, he brought in Damian Roden, who had worked with Speed at Bolton and gone on to work with a host of other clubs, developing a very good reputation in the field. Circumstances fell strangely to enable these two good friends to come and work together. Roden had taken a similar job with the Australian national team, only for a blood clot in his calf to prevent him from travelling long distances and force him to resign. When Speed came calling offering the same role, Roden viewed the chance to work with his good friend for his country as a 'no-brainer'.

The most noteworthy of Speed's appointments was arguably that of his assistant. Speed opted for Dutch football coach Raymond Verheijen, an unusual choice given the tendency of Wales managers to appoint predominantly Welsh backroom staff, or people they had played with or had previous experience of. Speed had none of that with Verheijen and simply picked him on reputation.

Wales left-back Neil Taylor speaks very highly of Speed's backroom staff, particularly Verheijen. 'They were massive to us because he brought in all the right people,' says Taylor, who came up through the age levels to make his full international debut in 2010. 'With Raymond he just brought him in because he knew how good he was at his job and nothing else. I think he'd worked with Craig [Bellamy] at Manchester City. Raymond was the type of character who was quite strict, well-spoken and I think that Dutch arrogance he had helped in instilling belief in us players. He definitely had that arrogance but he backed it up, he knew what he was doing with players. If somebody was a quick sprinter compared to someone with average pace he would tailor training for that person. Also tactically he knew a lot and you knew for Gary to have employed him that he must be a really good guy and he was.'

As for Speed's vision itself, it was very much in line with the vision of the Association at the time – modernisation and professionalism were the key words. Verheijen speaks in his own book *How Simple Can It Be?* about how Speed warned him of what he was getting himself into by coming on board with Wales, because the modern, professional set-up that Speed was desperate to create, was very much still in its infancy and needed a lot of work to get to where it needed to be. The player withdrawals during the Toshack era were a problem, as there was all sorts of talk of people pulling out with suspicious injuries, which is something Verheijen had also remarked upon in his book: 'Many players just came to the national team because of formalities and patriotism, but, didn't have the idea that they would ever be able to qualify for a European championship or World Cup. Some didn't come at all, or the coach of their club said: go use that international break as a holiday.'

The vision Speed had to change everything was broken down into six phases; six steps to go through that would result in Wales qualifying for, and performing well at the World Cup in Brazil in 2014. The chances of qualifying for Euro 2012 were practically non-existent, as Wales had lost three out of three qualifiers before he had taken charge, so Speed and his team treated their remaining qualifiers as practice games which could be used towards advancing their six-phase plan.

Phase one, which ran for most of Speed's first year, was to improve everything away from the pitch. Phase two, which ran from autumn 2011 to the end of winter 2012, saw the coaching staff focus on developing the offensive side of Wales' play. Phase three was developing the defensive aspect and phase four was to qualify for the 2014 World Cup. Phase five was the preparations for that tournament, and the sixth phase would be to maintain that level of preparation and performance for the tournament itself.

Wales striker Simon Church identifies the squad's very first meeting with Speed as a defining moment: "I think from the very first day, he got us in and told us exactly what he was going to change, what he wanted us to do and how much he believed in us and the aim, which was to qualify for Brazil. We all bought into it straight away and that moment really stuck with me where we as players just turned around and said, "Yeah, it is time for us to step up and really push for the next level now."'

Perhaps the biggest indicator of how Wales were going to look as team under Speed in terms of playing style was his choice of captain. Speed opted for 20-year-old Aaron Ramsey, a modern, industrious, creative midfielder. Ramsey is the sort of player who wants to take the corners before getting into the box to head them in.

From the outside looking in, it was clear early on that Speed had a vision. In Speed's first game in charge against the Republic of Ireland in the Carling Nations Cup, Craig Bellamy turned up to sit in the stands and support the team even though he couldn't play due to injury. He was, he confessed, making a point of showing everyone that he was on board, and that others should follow his example in making every effort to realise Speed's vision.

A 3–0 defeat for Wales in that game meant Speed wouldn't get his tenure off to the positive start everyone was longing for, perhaps understandably given that the manager only had one training session with his depleted group of players before this fixture. BBC Wales' Rob Phillips recalls his emotions travelling home after Wales' performance. 'We travelled back the day after the game,' says Phillips. 'I was in the airport and Speed came across to have a casual chat. He asked me what was up. I was quite down after another defeat. It wasn't anything against him at all, but we had just lost again and I told him that although I love my job, it is difficult to watch sometimes. He sat me down there and then and told me, "Listen, I've had a day with these players. We will get better," and he threw this passion at me with a look in his eyes and said, "Give me time, we'll get this sorted. I know what I want and I know how we're going to do it. Give us time, we're going to do something, you mark my words." I was surprised, because it was such a rousing conversation that made me believe, whether or not he was a success, he was going to give his all to ensure it went as well as it possibly could.'

Speed's coaching team tried to implement a new style of play right from the first game – which would later be described as the Welsh interpretation of Total Football – but understandably the team struggled with it. So in order to keep the players focused and believing in the system that they were trying to implement, Verheijen created a clip of certain periods of the game where the players had actually managed to execute the new philosophy Speed wanted from the team. It was only a four-minute spell, but the players had managed to do it. In his book *How Simple Can It Be?*, Verheijen explained: 'Up until then the players had looked at the problem as if they had to learn something new. After seeing that clip, they realised it was only a matter of extending four minutes to ninety minutes and then to ten qualification games. So more of the same. Maintaining something for longer is much easier than having to learn something new. After that the players couldn't claim they weren't able to do it. We had sent the football thinking in our players in the right direction.'

Continuing to use that method over the coming games was a great motivational tool and a source of reassurance for the players. It kept reminding them that they were improving and they could do what Speed and his team were asking them to do.

Building from the back, playing through the thirds, with width and pace in a 4–3–3, it was a very attractive brand of football, but it needed time to be developed properly. 'It was almost Total Football with the amount of passing we were doing,' explains midfielder Jack Collison. 'It was something Gary and Raymond implemented straight away, wanting us to play out from the back and have the confidence to get on the ball. I think the way they wanted us to play only helped the likes of Aaron Ramsey and Joe Allen because they were used to doing that for their clubs. It was a very brave decision because in the early days the results weren't quite there, but Gary was a massive character and he never lost sight of what he wanted to achieve and how he felt was the best way to go about it.'

Wales goalkeeper Wayne Hennessey admits that Wales struggled to get used to this style initially. 'We weren't used to it, so it took a while, but once we were into it we were almost untouchable,' he says. 'It was difficult to change because a lot of us were playing in the Championship then and not a lot of possession football is played there; it is all long, diagonal stuff into the channels. But we liked the new system a lot. We lost a few games trying to learn our limits and learn where we needed to tweak it, but that's part and parcel of football.'

Wales didn't stand a chance of turning themselves into the team they wanted to become if they couldn't convince their best players to turn up for the national side. Speed and his backroom staff had to create an environment where the players felt grateful to be selected, or at least felt like they weren't dropping their standards when they turned up for Wales duty. Part of creating that environment was going to the players' clubs and convincing them of the standards of the new set-up and how professional it was going to be. As Damian Roden explains, 'One of our main aims was to instil belief from the clubs that we would look after their players – which we did. We didn't have a single injury in the whole of Gary's tenure. We built relationships and broke down barriers with clubs by visiting them all and explaining our philosophy and what we wanted to achieve, which helped clubs release players – certainly the likes of Aaron Ramsey and Gareth Bale. We set the stall out with every single player that, even if they were injured, we wanted them to come down because we would be talking about the game plan, the philosophy, the method, and we wanted that togetherness. We wanted them all to come down and be involved and progress as a group. Everyone bought into that because under Gary's tenure there wasn't one single withdrawal from the squad – everyone, injured or not, turned up.'

According to those involved at the time, everything in terms of preparation, training facilities, evaluation of training camps was at a reasonable standard within the Wales set-up. But it wasn't where Speed wanted it to be if he was going to turn Wales into a real professional outfit with ambitions of qualifying for a tournament. He couldn't demand the best from his players without giving them the best in terms of what they had to work with. If Speed did that then his players would have no excuses and, having been instrumental as a player under Mark Hughes and having seen the benefits of that approach first-hand, he recognised the importance of it and set about changing the hotels, bringing in sports science experts and top coaches, changing how the team travelled, how they prepared physically and nutritionally, how they analysed games – everything. Wales striker Sam Vokes says this modernisation of the set-up was exactly what the squad needed. 'It took us onto a more professional angle,' says Vokes. 'I've always spoken highly of Toshack because he gave me my first cap, so I'm always grateful for that, but to move on to the next level I think we needed the behind the scenes stuff really and with Raymond, Osian and Damian coming in we were certainly shown a different side of the game to what we'd seen before. They were a huge part of our success, obviously Speed was the head of that set-up but the backroom staff were brilliant. We started doing technical meetings analysing opponents, unit meetings for the strikers, midfielders and defenders – stuff we'd never done before – and it gave us a much broader understanding of the game and how the team wanted to play and Raymond directed a lot of that with Osian, they were definitely key to how well we did.'

The team spirit was building up behind the scenes, too. Most of these players would have grown up watching Gary Speed on the television captaining Wales, so he immediately had their respect and admiration for that reason. Speed capitalised on that by repaying their respect in kind. Making Ramsey captain clearly showed the younger players that he had the utmost faith in them, but he worked hard on creating an atmosphere of unity within the camp by doing the little things like getting all of his players and staff together one night and teaching them the national anthem. Speed wanted to make everyone feel like they were in this together and, talking to the players about it, is clear he succeeded in creating that tightknit dynamic.

Of course, implementing so many changes was going to take time. The first phase of Speed's six-phase plan accounted for six months, which is an incredibly long spell in football. With results taking a while to materialise – Speed would lose four of his first five games in charge – supporters and journalists confessed to me that they did doubt whether or not anything would actually change under Speed. But those within the FAW were adamant that this was something that was expected given the extent of the changes that Speed wanted to undertake. 'Invariably it takes time,' explains CEO Jonathan Ford, 'especially in a scenario where you were going from John to Gary, from someone who was playing in the '70s to someone who was playing not long before he took the job. When Gary came in it was all about performance, sports science, preparation, making sure you have the data from the players, driving that team ethic, and that took time. It's not like a new manager comes in and it all changes, our game is different. Five games sounds like a lot, but everything is so much more gradual in international football. We only have a maximum of 12 games a year, so our timelines are considerably longer. We all acknowledged that it was going to be a longer-term thing.'

It was outlined to the players from day one that, internally at least, there would be no pressure in the opening six months to get results, as it was all about putting the tools in place to ensure Wales got to their end goal, which was reaching Brazil 2014 and the players were all on board with that. But it was surely testing for Speed as a new manager to be able to keep these players' spirits up throughout the first few months, to convince them to believe in the idea that change was afoot if they were patient and did everything he asked them to do to achieve it. In terms of management style, he had learnt a lot from the men he had worked under in his playing days. Roden, who also worked with Sam Allardyce and Mark Hughes during his career, says that there were striking similarities between Speed's management style and those of the managers he had played under. 'He definitely embraced everything that would get that extra advantage that Sam Allardyce was renowned for,' recalls Roden. 'I saw that in him for sure. I think Gary's time at Bolton extended his career by a few years, to be honest, because of the work we were doing with regards to his recovery, nutrition and Pilates and so on. Gary definitely brought that into management with him because he was adamant that Wales were going to be at the cutting edge. In terms of Mark's influence, Mark is very calm under pressure, very collected in how he approaches things. He's very structured and I could see that straight away in how Gary went about his business.' In addition to those qualities, John Carver noted how Speed's ability as a man-manager and a motivator was very similar to that of Sir Bobby Robson, under whom he'd played at Newcastle United.

The first competitive game for Speed, against England in Cardiff, would see him begin to use the qualifying games as practice games to develop his philosophy. Although it was unreasonable to expect miracles from Speed in terms of his team's performance on the pitch so early on, everyone would see further glimpses of the style of play that the manager wanted his team to play going forward, despite the absence of talisman Gareth Bale who pulled out with an injury in the days building up to the game. Osian Roberts confesses it was a risk to try a new approach in such circumstances. 'We knew that we could get thumped trying to implement our new style of play,' says Roberts, 'but it was a risk worth taking to put the building blocks in place for a sustainable structure. We were prepared to take the hit and we did as we lost 2–0, but the problem stemmed from our midfielders coming too deep in build-up which was inviting pressure onto us in our own half, so we could never get out easily. We needed to go through that though, so we could show the players where they were going wrong, where they needed to work on and we worked on addressing that over time.'

In light of both Bale's absence and the defeat, which was sealed quickly after Frank Lampard and Darren Bent scored inside the opening 15 minutes, there was a feeling of deflation in some quarters after just two games, as some supporters felt there were very few tangible signs of progress. But the Bale injury was another significant turning point for Wales under Speed. It seemed insignificant at the time but in hindsight it was very much the opposite, because media outlets reported that Bale had been injured during Wales training on the Wednesday before the game, even though Bale hadn't trained that day as he was having a scan on what Wales knew was a hamstring injury that he'd picked up while he was playing for his club the previous weekend. Wales responded to this misinformation strongly by contacting Tottenham Hotspur to set the record straight, as did Verheijen by responding himself to the news on Twitter, calling the media who had leaked the inaccurate news 'incompetent amateurs'. The way with which Wales defended themselves in this matter and came out strongly against the media, as well as the fact that Wales were the ones who had sent Bale for the aforementioned scan in the first place and recommended that he not train to avoid aggravating the injury, showed everyone – players, clubs, segments of the media – that Wales weren't messing around any more, and greatly helped all of those parties buy into the regime being implemented by Speed and his team. Furthermore, Speed's post-match comments throughout the campaign would be key to keeping his players' spirits up. Speaking to the BBC he said: 'Hopefully we keep that spirit that we saw in the second half and keep trying to play football – I think it's very, very encouraging. It was obviously a disappointing start. We're a young team and haven't won many games recently and to go a goal behind was a body-blow and it took us the rest of the first half to recover from that. Hopefully one or two years down the line when we're a better team, we'll look back and say we learned a lot from this game.'

Speed's resilience and unwavering belief in his vision was one of his key strengths. For Iwan Roberts these characteristics would become a defining memory of Speed. 'There was a bit of stick flying about, but Gary never flinched,' says Roberts. 'He stood in his technical area for the whole 90 minutes. He never hid. He could have taken the easy option and sat in the dugout away from it all but he didn't, he took it on the chin. He knew the team wasn't playing well, that they weren't the finished product, but he wasn't going to hide or shy away – he was more of a man than that and he stood there and took a lot of abuse. That was Gary, he was a fighter.'

Nonetheless, four games into Speed's reign the first win finally came. Wales beat Northern Ireland 2–0 in the Carling Cup of Nations in May, in front of a paltry crowd of roughly 600 people, an attendance that the game is more often remembered for than Wales' success in the match. Northern Ireland offered no attacking threat at all, as Speed's team dominated and probably should have won by more than they did. 'We knew we had a good group of players,' says Wales midfielder Jack Collison, 'and we knew that if we could get it all together then eventually the results would come, and never once did Gary Speed get downhearted. He knew that somewhere in there, there was a team capable of winning games. Maybe it took longer than expected, but if you look at other managers previously and Chris Coleman since then the same thing happened to a lot of them, they had slow starts too. We knew winning internationals wasn't too far around the corner and we proved that eventually.'

The next fixture was a home game to Australia at the Cardiff City Stadium in August and, after getting the monkey off the back in the previous game with a win, the perception was that it was going to be another win for Wales and that it would all spark from there into something really special. Certainly all of the evidence pointed towards this being a good game for Wales, as Speed named a full-strength side for the first time in his tenure, demonstrating the success that he had in changing the culture within the squad. With a fair amount of pre-season rust to contend with, though, Wales were not at their fluent best and ultimately didn't live up to the hype that others had set around the game. A timid first half performance saw Wales succumb to a 1–0 half-time deficit thanks to a goal in the 44th minute by Tim Cahill. It was soon 2–0 in the second half and it looked like the game was over, until the last quarter of an hour where something sparked Wales into life and everything seemed to look like it should do. The passing became quick and incisive. Wales looked good in possession and created chances, and the Dragons got their rewards with a goal from Darcy Blake to make it 2–1. It was too little, too late, though, as 2–1 is how it stayed.

Having been positive this far, for the first time you could sense that Speed was getting frustrated with his side's lack of progress when he spoke to the media after the Australia game. 'I learnt that we have not progressed as much as I thought we had,' he told the cameras. 'You can't give away two goals to sides like that because you rarely get back in it. We tried but it was too late. I was angry at half-time. They are all good players and they did not do themselves justice. We are building. We are trying to progress and get to the next step which is getting people into the positions to create chances. To get Bale, Bellamy and Ramsey into the game, we had been doing it well in training but it's different against a quality side like that. It shows how much we have to do. It's given everyone a kick up the backside. We need to knuckle down and improve.'

Speed's words would prove to have a resounding effect on everyone going forward, as Wales would win four of their next five games, against very tough opposition. Much like Rob Phillips' account of his conversation with Speed in the airport after Speed's first game, *Sgorio* producer Gary Pritchard notes how Speed's thoughts on this performance had a similar impact on him. 'For me, Australia was the turning point,' says Pritchard, 'because after every other game he said the same thing, that everyone knew where they needed to improve and that they were stepping in the right direction. But after Australia he came to do his post-match interviews and he was furious, absolutely furious. He hadn't been like that with the team before. He was so angry – things he'd been praising the players for before he was now saying they hadn't made enough progress in those areas. For the first time everyone saw that Speed knew when he had to be tough with all of these players and from that point onwards everyone was quite confident he'd do a good job.'

The defeat prompted calls for Speed to be sacked, perhaps understandably so after one win in five games, but much better times were to come. The Montenegro game the following month signified the first game of Speed's second phase. No more was the sole focus on developing the infrastructure and disregarding results. From now on the results mattered, and his team responded magnificently. Wales changed formation marginally going into this next run of games, sticking with a 4–3–3 but playing with one defensive pivot, instead of the two that they'd been using up to this point. Bale moved to the right wing from the left, and despite a wobbly start against Montenegro, where the defence was caught napping a couple of times, Wales showed real promise in attack for a good portion of the match. Ramsey, Bale and Bellamy all looked rampant in the 20 minutes before and after half-time, as Speed's men flew into a 2–0 lead. A very nervy finish to the match, following the substitution of Ramsey for the more defensive-minded Andrew Crofts, saw Wales having to weather a lot of pressure, and Stevan Jovetić pulled one back for the away side. But Wales held out to secure the win – their first of the qualifying campaign, and only their second win under Speed after six games.

They had looked much better in this game and everything was looking very promising. Afterwards, the manager told the BBC how proud he was that the team had come out of the other side of the difficult run they had endured. 'It's very pleasing,' said Speed. 'We've done a lot of work over the last six months to develop what we want, introducing the playing style, and sometimes we have to forfeit the result in order to show the players what we want. If we want to be successful we've got to do something special and this might mean you have to take two steps back to take a step forward, which is what we've done over the last six months. So I'm glad that the players have got their reward for that here. We've been trying to get the ball down and play it, pass and move, because we're comfortable on the ball and I think some of the passing tonight showed that. The whole team, I'm pleased for them. It's been tough having to stamp your authority in a new post at times but I think tonight they've shown that they're bearing the fruits of all of the hard work.'

Ramsey said after the Montenegro game that confidence was flowing within the side ahead of their next game – a monumental clash with their rivals England at Wembley. In terms of their standings in the qualifying group it wasn't significant. England were running away with it, whereas

Wales had only just got their first win. But in terms of Wales' development over the last six months this game would be the biggest test of their progress.

Speed's men would lose the encounter 1–0, thanks to an early goal by Ashley Young, but Wales bossed possession and were very much in control for large periods. They also succeeded in keeping Wayne Rooney quiet. *The Telegraph* described him as 'being in a different postcode to his teammates'. Wales had Fabio Capello's men under real pressure towards the end, where only Robert Earnshaw's agonising miss had kept Wales from a thoroughly deserved point. It was such a strong performance from the Welsh that Capello apologised to the Wales coaching staff after the game, because they were unable to get the point he felt they deserved. Everything had come full-circle. Despite the defeat, Speed and his team had been vindicated in their belief that the way they were doing things was correct. Six months previously they hadn't been able to keep pace with the Republic of Ireland in Dublin, but now they'd just gone to Wembley and been exceptionally unlucky to come away without any points from a game against a very strong England side.

Earnshaw, obviously devastated to not have scored the equaliser that Wales deserved, was very positive in his post-match comments to UEFA, stating that this performance and the confidence the team could take from it would result in Wales taking 'five or six steps forward' in their development. With qualifiers against Switzerland and Bulgaria to come and then a friendly against Norway, everything pointed towards Speed's first year ending on an exceptionally strong note.

The media noted how Speed looked much more comfortable within himself following the defeat to England. Chris Wathan of Wales Online recalls the more buoyant mood within the camp before Wales' next game with Switzerland. 'He was getting great comfort in what he was doing around the Switzerland home game,' says Wathan. 'You sensed by that stage that he was very comfortable with where he was at the time and what he wanted to do. He always had a drop of humour about him, but there was more to it this time, he seemed more relaxed, cracking more jokes and being more comfortable around the press and you could see that embodied in the players as well, who had embraced it all and looked happy being around the place again.'

That positivity translated onto the pitch, as Wales were rampant in their final three games of the year: a 2–0 win over Switzerland, with goals from Bale and Ramsey; a 1–0 win away to Bulgaria, thanks again to a goal by Bale, and a 4–1 thrashing of Norway at the Cardiff City Stadium thanks to goals by Bale, Bellamy, and a two-minute brace from substitute Sam Vokes. It was blatantly obvious that everything was working. The likes of Speed, Bellamy and Ramsey had insisted that things were going to start working, that Wales would be a real outfit when it all turned around, and they were finally doing that. The results proved it. From four losses in five, Wales had moved to four wins in five, vaulting themselves from 117th in the international rankings after the Australia defeat to 45th after the win over Bulgaria. And all the while playing great attacking football. Iwan Roberts recalls that he was 'delighted' for his friend Speed. 'He'd persevered,' says Roberts. 'He'd worked hard, he'd got the players to believe in what he was trying to achieve and the way he was trying to achieve it. It doesn't happen overnight, but it just goes to show if you persevere and put all the hard work in, show you're honest on and off the pitch, you reap the rewards. We weren't just winning games, we were doing it with a certain style, a type of performance we hadn't seen from a Welsh team for a very, very long time.'

All of this though, the performances on the pitch, the adulation from the fans, the love for the game and the team again in Wales – the bandwagon filling up, if you like – only added to the overwhelming sense of tragedy a few weeks later when the terrible news broke of Gary Speed's passing. Never mind what it meant for the team in a sporting sense, on a basic human level Speed's death had touched so many people, evidenced by the plethora of tributes that poured in. He gave everything to his country in any way he could, and his time in charge reminded everyone that Wales could be a success again on the international footballing stage.

We'd all seen the potential for it when Toshack had brought through all of the players that he did, but under Speed Wales finally saw it all pull together with five excellent performances in his last five games in charge. By modernising and by restoring pride and professionalism to the squad, by adopting an attractive playing style, he set a standard that everyone would expect to be adhered to in future years for Welsh football.

The day Gary Speed left us was so surreal. Personally I've never experienced another day like it, and the hole it left in people's hearts was plain for all to see – thousands of people asking for games to be called off, former teammates and friends in tears, everyone just devastated by the tragic passing of one of the game's icons. The following tributes are essentially a drop in the ocean compared to the millions that were left in his memory:

Damian Roden: 'He was an absolute legend in every way – he achieved so much in his career, it was unbelievable. When he finished playing he held the record for the most Premier League appearances and that in itself was a massive achievement, but the way he conducted himself and the way he approached a conversation with anyone and everyone was like someone who was just starting out in professional football, not of someone who had achieved what he had achieved. He was the same as a manager. He had so much time for everybody. Whether they wanted to speak to him, wanted his autograph, he had time for everybody – an absolute gem of a guy.'

Neville Southall: 'You speak to any football fan about Speed and they won't have a bad word to say about him. Everywhere he went people loved him, because he gave everything to the game. If things went wrong he wasn't happy. He could sulk at times, be grumpy, be stubborn, but all because he was a winner and a class player. He looked like the real deal. He carried himself in the right way and whatever he said he was going to do he did – he kept his word on everything. I watched him play many times. I played with him, played against him, and he was a fabulous footballer, but I maintain that he doesn't get the credit he deserves. I can't think of any players who could do what he did, I wouldn't compare him to anyone, because he was better than everyone at what he did.'

Shay Given: 'Even now talking about him is difficult. It's been nearly four years and this is the first time I've talked about him since he's gone. It's very difficult even to speak about him and to talk about him as if he's not here, because he was one of my best friends in football and I foresaw in the future that we could have worked together as coaches. We had all of these plans with each other. There isn't a defining memory, but he's always there in my mind. Wherever he is he still seems to be standing next to me. I think that can only be a good thing. He made such an impression on my life that he's never far away from my thoughts.'

Neil Taylor: 'Whenever you talk to people who played with Gary Speed, everyone says he had that aura about him. Whenever he walked into a room he had that aura. I'll always remember the respect Craig Bellamy had for him, thinking if he had so much respect for Gary then he must be some man. Gary was a passionate Welshman who helped bring that passion back to the side and his passing away was terrible for us. I remember the game here against Villa that morning and it was a massive shock. It didn't sink in, to be honest. It didn't even begin to sink in until after the game that evening. You naturally think of the family at that time. It must have been incredibly difficult for them.'

Sam Vokes: 'It was a tough time for all of us, because it was only a couple of weeks before he passed away that we were playing Norway and Speed was talking about the next steps and where we were going and looking to the future and so on and we were all really excited for that, but what happened obviously meant it was an incredibly sad time. That game was the last time I spoke to Gary Speed, he was buzzing with the performance and it was a great night and really epitomised how exciting a time it was for Welsh football.'

Rob Phillips: 'It struck me about his influence at his clubs on the day he died. We had to come in and do a tribute to him for the next few days. I'll never forget the phone call I had that morning, half-nine, ten o'clock in the morning. I was at home because there was a Swansea game that day. I wasn't working on it so I didn't need to be there, but I got that call and went straight into work. Speaking all day to people who knew him – Rob Earnshaw, Howard Wilkinson – everywhere he went, there was so much respect for him from those places and beyond on that day. The various tributes were incredible, I don't think we'll see anyone like Gary Speed again – he had no enemies, no detractors. Everybody loved him.'

Gary Speed's death was absolutely terrible. There's no other way to put it. It shook everyone who had ever heard of him, watched him or met him, to the core. I don't know how you summarise a man like that. I've tried here to give my own brief tribute to the career he had and the person he was, but we all had our own memories of him and it's a shame I couldn't speak to more people who knew him, because it would have made for a much better account of the man himself. Finding a word or a quote or a moment to encapsulate just what Gary Speed stood for is an impossible task. He improved everything he went and put his heart into, the clubs he played for, the country he loved to play for, the people he met in day-to-day life, everything. How can you encapsulate a man like that?

Rob Phillips hits the nail on the head by summarising his legacy: 'He's the record outfield player for us with 85 caps. He was a great player, so consistent. A great character. And I think if I had to define him I'd say this: whenever Speed went on the pitch as a player, captain or a manager, he commanded respect. He didn't demand it, he commanded it because he didn't have to ask for it. He was just Gary Speed.'

CHAPTER 5

The Hilton Hotel, John Lennon Airport – 14 January 2011

'I knew within five minutes of sitting down in a room with
Gary, that this was a guy I had to work with'

RAYMOND VERHEIJEN, WALES ASSISTANT MANAGER, 2011–12

BEHIND EVERY GREAT manager is a great team; not just on
the pitch, but away from it. Whether it be a manager's family,
friends, their assistant manager, the kit-man, the physio,
technical directors – whoever. You'll have a tough job making
it as a manager if you don't have that core group behind you to
help make the important decisions and help with the day-to-day
running of a professional set-up. One of Gary Speed's key goals
was to modernise the Wales set-up, to create an environment
that was on a par with Premier League clubs in terms of player
care, player preparation and so on – to make it somewhere that
all of the selected players looked forward to going to. Of course,
he couldn't do this on his own – great managers know their
strengths but they also know their weaknesses and therefore
hire individuals to become members of their backroom staff
with the specific intention of covering those weaknesses.

A key appointment of Speed's was Dutch coach Raymond
Verheijen as his assistant manager. Verheijen is well known for
his tactical expertise, organisational know-how and immense
understanding in the field of player fitness. Craig Bellamy in
particular hired Verheijen personally to develop his fitness
whilst on club duty. Verheijen is most famous for his work with
his compatriot Guus Hiddink, when the pair took a number

of 'sleeping giants' as Verheijen calls them – Russia and South Korea – and helped them realise their potential at international tournaments. Verheijen was a key part of the Speed set-up, and in researching this book I spoke to him extensively regarding his time working with Gary Speed. Here is how Verheijen himself reflected on the experience:

JT: What did you think of Gary Speed as a person and a professional?

RV: As a professional I think he was, for his generation, one of the most forward-thinking players, always looking for new things to keep his body fit, which is one of the reasons why he kept playing for so long and stayed at the top level for so long. He was very disciplined and very open-minded, looking at things like nutrition, injury-prevention etc. So besides the fact that he was a great player, he was also extremely professional.

JT: How much did you know of the Wales set-up before you came on board?

RV: What I knew about Wales was mainly what I'd seen from them in the games they'd played against Holland. They had been in the same qualifying group a number of times. When I was approached, one of the things that I've learned from my mentor Guus Hiddink is that it's not so much the current level of the team that is important when deciding whether or not to join the team. It's all about the potential, because you can work with a top team, a team already performing at the highest level, but the potential left to exploit is relatively small which means they probably won't maintain their success, so then you shouldn't work with that team. While on the other hand, a team can be performing at relatively low level with a lot of unfulfilled potential; if you compare the two it's obviously better to work with the latter. Hiddink and I did this with South Korea in 2002 for the World Cup as well as with Russia in Euro 2008 – those teams were sleeping giants. Underachievers. If you analyse Wales in 2011, then you could see that there was a lot of potential there.

JT: How did it come about that you joined Wales?

RV: I met Gary on Friday, 14 January 2011 at John Lennon Airport in Liverpool in the Hilton hotel and I started that conversation with a very open mind. I remember that within five minutes, I already knew that I wanted to work with Gary. My first impression of Gary was extremely positive, because normally when you work with young and inexperienced coaches they talk a lot but they don't say a lot, if you understand what I mean. They talk a lot. They are full of energy and ambitious, but what they say goes all over the place and is unstructured. With Gary he was a young and inexperienced coach, but immediately I recognised that he knew exactly what he wanted – he didn't necessarily know how he wanted to do it but he knew what he wanted – and he was very structured and clear, which is very uncharacteristic of the inexperience he had as a manager at that time. If a young, inexperienced manager, like Gary was then, is already so clear and so structured in what he wants to do, then that obviously means he has a lot of potential to become very successful.

JT: Did he continue to impress you when you eventually worked together for Wales?

RV: Yes, what was most impressive about him was how relaxed he always was, especially in the beginning when it was quite tough and there was some questioning about the way things were going; the way he stayed calm was very impressive. I could see the respect that the players had for him which was also impressive. At the same time though, he was always very humble – wherever he went he signed autographs for everybody, and I mean everybody. I've worked with a lot of top coaches and a lot of top players and let me tell you, that isn't common at all, so it was a testament to the kind of man he was.

JT: What was the biggest challenge Wales faced at the start of the Speed tenure?

RV: The biggest challenge was that everybody showed up, because Wales is a very small country so the group of quality players is relatively small. If you only have 14 or 15 players who are capable of playing international football and five or six of them don't show up then you have a problem. If five players don't show up for Spain or Germany then they just pick five others and still win, but for Wales at that time if the same thing happened then it made it incredibly difficult for everyone to deal with – it's almost certain that you aren't going to win. So the first challenge was to create an environment where the coaching staff no longer had to feel grateful for the players showing up, but instead the players began to feel grateful for being selected.

JT: How did the foundations put in place enable you to extract the potential these players had?
RV: Well I think that the biggest reason was that we had a very structured and detailed plan with different phases. When we started in February we had communicated those phases to the players and all phases had specific objectives – going from phase to phase we were very clear and very structured, so it was very easy for the players to follow what we wanted. The other thing is that it was also very clear to the players that we meant business, that we would not accept 99 per cent, so as well as changing the environment we also changed the players' way of thinking which enabled them to realise their potential.

JT: Of course, as a result of this the squad developed a real sense of togetherness and self-belief...
RV: Yes, and I think that's because we knew what we wanted and we knew how we wanted it. Phase One was to make sure that everything was perfect off the pitch, outside the pitch, and that phase was from February to August. Phase Two was from September until November and that was making sure that everything would be perfect on the pitch. In that second phase we jumped from 117th to 45th in the FIFA world rankings. If your objective in the second phase is to ensure that everything is going well on the pitch, then I think that the rankings do the talking for us there really, in showing that we got it right. There were no favourites in terms of the players – the togetherness of the team was one of the strengths and was a key reason for why we improved.

JT: Losing four of the first five games, there must have been some concerns there?

RV: No I wasn't worried, because we had to sort things out away from the pitch first. If you want your players to do everything perfect on the pitch, you have to sort everything away from it out first, because it's impossible to demand perfection from the guys on the pitch otherwise. After August we began to pay attention to everything on the pitch – we knew our achievements before that were not going to be top class and was something that we accepted in advance. Only from September onwards did we demand top class on the pitch.

We were never worried that it wouldn't work out – sorting everything out off the pitch first made perfect sense, because trying to develop things off and on the pitch at the same time isn't possible. If you're not focusing 100 per cent on developing the playing style because you are focusing on other things, then you are going to lose more games anyway. The only moment you have to be worried is if you focus on the playing style entirely and you still lose, then you have a problem. If you focus on things off the pitch and you lose then it doesn't matter, because losing isn't the consequence of what you're doing at that moment because you are focusing on other things – better hotels, training facilities, training sessions etc.

People say that after September the results got better and ask what could have been had events not unfolded in the tragic way that they did, but you can't look at it that way because the qualifying group for the World Cup in Brazil was exceptionally difficult. It's impossible to say when you are in a group with Belgium and Croatia that we would have qualified. We might have. You can't say for sure though. What you can say is that for 2016, especially with the top two qualifying and the third reaching the play-offs, there would have been a great chance and the team is proving that at the moment.

JT: In the form of yourself, Osian Roberts, Damian Roden and others, Speed had great backroom staff – how would you summarise the importance of the staff as a whole to Gary Speed's success?

RV: The person who turned it around is Gary Speed because he's the one who brought the backroom staff together. Despite the fact that the backroom staff had done a great job, Gary is the man who is ultimately responsible for that. One of his biggest strengths, talking of things that were impressive about him, was that he knew his strengths but he also knew his weaknesses and he understood that he had to surround himself with people who could compensate for his weaknesses. Normally managers surround themselves with weak yes-men, people who are loyal but are yes-men, but Gary surrounded himself with strong characters which again proves that he was a very strong and stable person, because you have to be strong to surround yourself with strong people.

JT: Many people praised your contribution, but what do you think you brought to the set-up?
RV: It's always better if other people talk about what I bring to the set-up of course, it's not my place to. One of the characteristics in Dutch football is that people coach you about what you do well, instead of your weaknesses. It's very tempting for a coach to talk about weaknesses and things that go wrong but, although in doing so a coach would have the best intentions, by constantly doing that, psychologically players are constantly thinking about what they're doing wrong which has a negative effect on their confidence. What we did was to constantly coach about the things that were going right, not coaching in terms of mistakes but in terms of solutions, and as a result your players feel more confident.

JT: Did you want to succeed Speed as Wales manager?
RV: No I didn't and I never said that. I never said I wanted to be the Wales manager – I don't have my Pro Licence so it's impossible to be a manager. The reason I don't have a Pro Licence is because my ambition isn't to be a manager. What I actually said was Osian Roberts and I should lead the team, because Osian is Welsh and he has his Pro Licence. Obviously people accused me of wanting the job and the reason why I never reacted to those accusations is because I felt sorry for those people, because I never applied for the job and I already knew that it was impossible for me to get it.

JT: In the round, where does your time with Wales rank among the other roles you've taken on?

RV: The Wales project is one of the fondest memories of all of the things I've done. I've done four World Cups and four European Championships. I've worked with top clubs, Barcelona, Manchester City, Chelsea, whatever and despite all these high-profile things that I've done the project with Wales is one of the nicest things I've done and I'm not just saying that; neither am I saying that because of the tragic ending. I'm saying it because thankfully my wife was the one that made me aware of how happy I was in the role in September 2011, because my family was in the hotel when we were preparing for the England game and thankfully she made me aware of the fact that I was really enjoying the work and how special it was to me.

I don't know if it comes across in writing but, having spoken to Verheijen, I'm not surprised he's been as successful as he has been throughout his career. We didn't really touch on the way things ended between himself and the Welsh set-up, but it's clear how much he admired one of the most important figures in the country's football history, Gary Speed.

Raymond spoke in a calm, confident manner – almost arrogant, in a good way – which was a theme reflected within the Wales side at that time; they were calm and confident in the way they played and had real belief for the first time in a long time. Gary Speed was obviously a huge part in instigating that, but Verheijen, Roberts, Roden and the rest of the set-up behind the scenes played their part too.

CHAPTER 6

The Total Game Plan and a Vision of Success – The FAW Strategy, 2012

'This association was a bit of a sleeping opportunity and it was really important that we just started modernising, becoming more dynamic, showing more ambition.'

JONATHAN FORD, CEO FOOTBALL ASSOCIATION OF WALES

'THE MESSAGE HAS been clear on the badge for years. *Gorau Chwarae Cyd Chwarae* (The Best Play Is Team Play). Our messages are clear; greater team work, better communication, a longer-term perspective through evolution and winning more. Included in our vision of success is a Welsh way of playing and qualification for a major tournament. Also, a Premier League and domestic competitions that have a strong identity within the Welsh sporting psyche. It is also important to be progressive and promote a forward thinking, modern and high profile FAW.'

Those were the sentiments of FAW CEO Jonathan Ford on 26 January 2012, at St David's Hotel in Cardiff where individuals from all corners of Welsh football had assembled for the unveiling of the FAW's new strategy for the Welsh game; a strategy that was to be gradually implemented over the next few years.

FAW strategies are documents that are released by the Association every few years to outline how they want to develop the game in Wales in the near future. These documents are put together by a host of people involved with Welsh football, but it is possible to see the influences of individual managers at the time they are written – in this case, Gary Speed.

We've looked in detail in this book at how Speed, along with Osian Roberts and others, came up with a plan to change Welsh football for the better and, while Roberts and Chris Coleman are still implementing and evolving that plan to this day, the FAW's 2012 strategy is an example of how the FAW's, Speed's and Coleman's vision for the game in Wales aligned. We'll touch briefly on some examples of where one can see the 2012 strategy being implemented in Welsh football further on in the book, but the rest of this chapter in particular will be dedicated to giving a broad overview of what the strategy is about and what steps needed to be taken to improve the game throughout Wales.

The strategy is comprehensive. It covers every aspect of the game in Wales and how it must be developed. However, you hear of these documents all the time. The key thing about these strategies is that they only work if you believe in them and have the patience to allow them to succeed – as demonstrated by the fact that words like belief, passion, pride, spirit, determination and resilience are very prominent within it. You don't have to look any further than the last World Cup winners to see what implementing and believing in a strategy can do for you. Germany developed their vision to change football at the turn of the millennium and were typically efficient in rolling it out, improving year upon year domestically and internationally at all levels, to the point where the men's national side won the 2014 World Cup. The target was different for Wales, obviously, with qualification the aim, but the point is that there's a precedent to show these strategies are worthwhile if the nation believes in them.

Contrast this with other countries which are constantly talking about trying new initiatives but perhaps not giving them the time they need to flourish, nor the leaps of faith they might need to make them work, and it isn't hard to see why patience is a crucial factor. It speaks wonders of the quality of Wales' strategy that ever since Speed and Roberts came in, and most recently of course Chris Coleman, and their visions have

Wales vs Russia, 2003. After a tremendous start to the group from Wales, momentum fell away and tactics were sussed out as Sparky's men went out of the play-offs with a whimper.

Tasked with bringing in the next generation, Wales lost a lot of fans during John Toshack's tenure, but they came back in their droves once the players he unearthed found their feet in the years that followed.

Photographs: © David Rawcliffe, Propaganda Photo

Charismatic, courageous, a legend. Toshack started the essential rebuilding process, but Gary Speed was the man who made the nation believe in Welsh football again.

The bravest of them all, Chris Coleman faced the immensely difficult task of living up to the excitement and the incredibly high standard set by his best friend, Gary Speed.

Paying tribute to one the game's legends. One of the most surreal experiences ever for Wales supporters, but Speed's work would never be forgotten in light of the successes that lay ahead.

Losing 6–1 to Serbia, this was the wake-up call Chris Coleman's Wales needed. An embarrassing defeat, Serbia served to kick-start Welsh football's rebuilding process following the limbo it found itself in.

The rain, the rivalry, the rocket. Bale's wonder-strike to seal victory versus Scotland would be particularly significant in helping Coleman turn his team's fortunes around in the months to come.

In his final act as a Wales player, Craig Bellamy helped Chris Coleman's side end their qualifying campaign with a 1–1 draw against Belgium in Brussels that catalysed Wales' future success.

The margins between disaster and success were never finer in this campaign than they were in Andorra. Fortune found Wales again and we should have known from there that this campaign would be historic.

Together Stronger. The fans and the players lauding each other on the first of many occasions throughout this campaign.

Israel 0–3 Wales. Coleman's men were ruthless as they annihilated the group leaders in Haifa, with Ramsey, Robson-Kanu and Bale playing a key role in putting Israel to the sword.

The Dragons slayed the Devils as the world's most expensive player scored one of Wales' most important goals on the way to securing a 1–0 win over Belgium in Cardiff.

Despite being on the brink of history, Wales' men maintained their focus until they'd achieved the holy grail and qualified for the European Championships.

Fifty-eight years is an unbelievably long time to wait, but the celebrations in Cardiff, three days after qualification was sealed, were absolutely worth the wait!

been unveiled, we've seen some of the other British nations duplicate aspects of Wales' framework in their countries, such as England's DNA programme, unveiled in December 2014, which is very similar to Wales' player pathway development programme that was unveiled years before.

UEFA's Welsh football correspondent Mark Pitman notes how crucial the Toshack era was to be in terms of what was to come from Wales' player pathway. 'It was the first time that a proper international pathway from youth to senior football had been implemented by Wales,' explains Pitman, 'as Brian Flynn was appointed to lead all of the intermediate teams. However, this approach was taken with the primary aim of fast-tracking young players through to the senior squad, unlike the pathway described in the 2012 strategy which has much more emphasis on ensuring youth players are developed with the same tactical approach and philosophy as the senior side. The subsequent progression of players like Gareth Bale and Aaron Ramsey meant that Toshack's successors benefited greatly from the experience they had gained under him ahead of their teenage years.'

The first thing the 2012 strategy focused on was an emphasis on changing perceptions. For far too long the success of Welsh football had been judged on the men's national side, which was unfair considering that the English FA in the 1980s, 1990s and 2000s, in particular, had been constantly praised for the quality of its domestic football teams, despite the fact that their national side was underachieving. Admittedly, having not qualified for a major international tournament since 1958 wasn't great but, on the other hand, football had been – and still is – comfortably the most watched and most played sport in Wales, with grassroots football players outnumbering rugby players three-to-one. In many areas Welsh football has led the way, or at least made a significant impact. The youth and women's teams have done very well; the country has been up with the best in coaching, safeguarding and refereeing and has attracted big tournaments and flagship matches such as the UEFA Super Cup (2014) and the Champions League final (2017).

The FAW decided that the best way to alter peoples' focus on the national side was to offer a clear analysis of the state of the game in Wales, as well as introducing 'joined-up thinking' to bring all of Welsh football together behind the common cause of improving the game as a whole. Welsh football, however, like football everywhere, has struggled recently with some key challenges. For instance, technology is fast becoming the new hobby of choice for youngsters. There are a host of new sports to play nowadays compared to years gone by quite apart from the general decline in school participation and exercise habit. Factor in the reality that Wales haven't qualified for a tournament for so long; the fact that rugby is (incorrectly) perceived as the country's most popular sport; that some of the country's top clubs play within the English system; and it soon becomes apparent that the challenges facing the FAW were and still are substantial.

Furthermore, while it's wrong that Welsh football has been judged on the strength of its national side, it is a fact that things haven't gone Wales' way in that regard as often as they should have done. Again, the word belief crops up here and the strategy makes a compelling argument as to why everyone should have more belief in Wales, using the 2010 World Cup as a case study.

Many excuses have been used over the years to give Wales the benefit of the doubt with regards to its underachievement on the men's international stage. The first is that Wales is a very small nation of around three million people, therefore it perhaps shouldn't be expected to reach the heights of other countries who have tens of millions of people to sample talent from. But Uruguay reached the semi-finals in 2010, and has won the World Cup twice, despite the fact that it is an even smaller a nation than Wales.

Other excuses were also proved invalid in South Africa. The false perception of Wales as a rugby nation was undermined by the fact that New Zealand (arguably even more of a rugby nation than Wales) went unbeaten in South Africa, even beating the then-world-champions Italy in their group. Then there's the notion that Wales struggles because it doesn't have a domestic league recognised as one of the best in Europe, which is contradicted by the fact that Italy and France had very successful leagues in 2010 and yet they went out at the group stages.

There have been examples throughout sporting history of psychology playing a role in the most successful teams, and it's clear at times in this strategy that one of its primary functions is to change the psychology towards Welsh football, building belief in the potential of the country at all levels of the game. The way to do this is by setting clear, tangible targets for the FAW to improve itself, involving the whole country in the successes that come with achieving those targets to make everyone feel part of a winning entity. This is particularly important in Wales given that the FAW has complicated relationships with its individual area associations. Each region of Wales is represented by regional councillors with the idea that this results in Wales being represented fairly – therefore involving them all in each other's successes is integral to build a sense of togetherness.

The question of how to achieve all of this is divided into four key subsections: Teamwork, Communication, Evolution and Winning More. The teamwork aspect is needed off the pitch as well as on it, and it's been clear to see as I've worked with some people at the FAW in writing this book that the team behind the team is absolutely top class. The key word here is inclusivity – with everyone singing from the same hymn sheet. This enables the development of an abiding 'Welsh Way' of working on and away from the field of play, creating a lasting legacy that all future regimes can adopt. Furthermore, when the time comes for the national team to take to the field, this inclusivity pays further dividends as this togetherness encourages the wider Welsh fan-base to get behind Wales' international teams by creating a real buzz in Cardiff, as well as in other cities around home matches. The FAW would go about doing this by creating direct links between the national game and the international scene by offering clubs incentives for ticket sales and playing U21 and Women's games at Welsh Premier League grounds.

With regard to communication the FAW, with the 2012 strategy, committed to developing a sense of openness by offering a 'no closed doors' approach to the Association's operations. The FAW is the third oldest Football Association in the game and some of the processes reflect that. Therefore the strategy made a commitment to looking at how the Association was run and how performance and expectations could be enhanced. After all, communication is what makes the successful teams tick and with this strategy the Association was aiming to understand exactly where they were at the time, and where they needed to be in order to set constant targets for improvement. With all of this in place, the key thing over time is to evolve it. We all know how quickly football can change and keeping up with that change is integral to any team or establishment that wants to be successful.

One of the key objectives the FAW implemented was to make Wales one of the best prepared national sides in world football. A cornerstone of this evolution was to create an environment where elite players wanted to come and perform to their best ability, by working actively with clubs to build relationships by maintaining awareness of and sensitivity to club regimes. Some high-profile figures within the game have been quite critical of players for shirking their responsibilities when it comes to attending national squads. Harry Redknapp, in particular, is one who noted it during his time at Tottenham. We've seen that Wales has suffered from the same problem. Whether that is because the players don't want to turn up, or the clubs don't want Wales to have the players, is purely speculative. To alleviate those concerns, the FAW, particularly since Gary Speed came in, worked very hard to develop not only their relationships with their players' clubs but the infrastructure within Wales training camps, in order to develop an environment that players and clubs are comfortable with attending.

Chris Whitley, chair of the international board that works extensively on these strategies, details the changes that took place to enable this. 'The technology we use now to monitor player health, fitness, tendencies and so on is unbelievable,' says Whitley. 'We have the same systems that Real Madrid use, which means that clubs are happy to send us players now, whereas before they wouldn't have been able to get all of the information we've got now.' A perfectly understandable situation considering Wales have the likes of Gareth Bale, who is valued at over £100m. The key ambition in this regard was to lay the best foundations off the pitch, with the aim that Wales would set a benchmark for sports medicine within football, offering medical, training and support for all of Wales, something previously alluded to by Verheijen.

Of course, as well as the sports science aspect and developing player wellbeing, work also needed to be done on developing the players' performance. The best way to do that was to develop the coaching set-up so that Welsh football had one integrated approach that ensured 'consistency of playing style and coaching messages throughout all levels and ages'. That focus on coach education has paid enormous dividends; for example the Welsh Football Trust has recently welcomed 350 coaches to its national coaching conference, attracting huge names to learn and teach its courses such as Tony Pulis, Roberto Martinez, Tim Sherwood, Patrick Vieira, as well as many others. One of the coaches who has been on courses organised by the Welsh Football Trust has told me, 'The coaching education in Wales is first class, absolutely first class. We had a record number of coaches at our recent national conference – 350 coaches! Unbelievable! Our coach education programme is second to none. The Welsh Football Trust is doing a tremendous job in terms of coaching education and player development.'

We've already touched on the pathway that John Toshack brought in during his tenure – this is something that Gary

Speed had a massive influence on during his time with the national side and is an integral part of the 2012 FAW strategy. FAW technical director Osian Roberts notes Speed's influence in this instance. 'When he got the job,' says Roberts, 'the first thing he said was that he wanted the first team to do what the under-16s were doing which was ideal for us, because we now have a system for developing the Welsh way of playing from younger age groups right up into the first team.' With Geraint Williams then brought in to manage other age groups, Wales again had a full player pathway to work with and this is one of the key features of this FAW strategy. Examples of the pathway programme's benefits can be seen in the senior squad today in the form of Emyr Huws, who captained the Wales team from the under-15s all the way through to under-21 level before joining up with the senior team. Roberts notes, 'When he came into the first team, Chris [Coleman] loved him because he fitted in straight away and slotted in without much work to be done to get him to understand our way.' This is by no means an indication that it works with every single player that gets into a youth squad, but it does show that the programme is an invaluable one for the future of the game in Wales.

Emyr Huws had this to say about his own pathway. 'At an early stage with the under-16s I was playing a year up, so playing in the Victory Shield when I was 15, and captaining the Victory Shield squad the following year,' said Huws. 'I played up a year with the under-17s as well, but I got a couple of injuries when I was 17/18 and missed a lot of football, so I was kind of playing catch-up, didn't play much for the under-19s and then played a few games for the under-21s. Everyone's transition is very different though, completely unique to each individual depending on how they grow, what luck they get with injuries and so on, but it generally goes very smoothly.'

FAW chief executive Jonathan Ford summarises the strategy perfectly. 'Changing the psychology around Welsh football was definitely a focal point of the strategy,' he says. 'The really interesting thing is that this Association at that time was a bit of a sleeping opportunity and ultimately it was just really important that we just started modernising, becoming more dynamic, showing more ambition. If there's one word that has changed everything that we have done here in my time it has been "ambition". We've been ambitious across everything that we do. We want to be the best, whether that's domestically, attracting major events, qualifying for major tournaments.'

Sitting here today, it is fair to say that Ford and the FAW succeeded in their ambitions. While there are a number of people, beyond the players, that grab the headlines, who are responsible for the brilliant position Welsh football finds itself in now, the 2012 strategy played a hugely significant part in the development of the game in Wales. By expanding and developing in great detail on the ideas brought in by some of the country's most influential footballing figures, it helped put Welsh football in a position to reach the situation it finds itself in today. Gary Speed's and Osian Roberts' vision is obvious throughout this strategy: the emphasis on sports science, the commitment to youth development as well as an ambition to build a long-lasting legacy for Welsh football.

It was a strategy developed by Jonathan Ford and the FAW, and influenced by the late great Gary Speed. His successor would be tasked with implementing this framework while replacing a man that most deemed irreplaceable. But while it showed the way the footballing powers in Wales wanted to take Welsh football in the immediate future, the game in Wales was still grieving after Speed's tragic death, and it would take a lot longer than anyone appreciated for those wounds to begin to heal.

PART 3

'We will always be indebted to Gary, but I think everyone needs to respect that it is Chris' team now and he is the manager and if we get to Euro 2016 it'll be Chris' achievement as a manager.'

OSIAN ROBERTS

CHAPTER 7

The perfect choice to take over from Gary Speed – Chris Coleman's unveiling

'I don't think anyone fully appreciated the difficulty of the circumstances at the time for Chris Coleman. I'm not sure some people do even now, four years on.'

CHRIS WATHAN, WALES ONLINE

IT SHOULDN'T HAVE to be said, but in case it does I'll say it anyway – pick the greatest manager you've ever seen, at the peak of his or her powers, and ask them to take on the Wales job after Gary Speed's tragic passing. No matter what challenges they'd overcome in their career, how good they were, how big an ego they had, whatever criteria made that manager great, they'd have all struggled immensely to fill the hole Speed left in Welsh football and take the side forward.

That's what Gary Speed's successor Chris Coleman was tasked with when he was named the new manager of the Wales team on 19 January 2012. It is fair to say that nobody wanted him to be in that job. That isn't at all a comment on Coleman as a manager. He has proven throughout his career that he is a top manager and the fans love him, not least for what he has done since coming in with Wales. It is simply the fact that everyone still wanted Speed in the dugout. Anything less than that wasn't good enough in the eyes of the fans. Circumstances meant that Wales fans were always going to be heartbroken in that respect, and that grieving process would take as long as it took, but Coleman was the right man to take the team forward, undoubtedly.

Having played against each other in the Welsh Cup final as ten year olds, Speed and Coleman were the closest of friends. When Coleman's Swansea took on Speed's Deeside back then, the former warned everyone in his dressing room of the latter's prowess – 'Watch that Speed, he's a damn good player!' On their journeys through football, these two kept finding each other at club trials or playing for the Wales youth teams, and eventually the senior team.

'They roomed together, played golf together, did everything together – they were really, really close,' says Iwan Roberts. 'For Coleman to come in under those horrific circumstances, I can't imagine how Chris must have felt going for that interview, being offered the job and then having to accept the job. Having said that, you couldn't wish for anybody better to pick up the pieces after the tragic events that happened with Gary. There was a legacy that Gary started and his good mate now was chosen to go on, keep it going and complete it.'

Kit Symons, the man chosen as Coleman's assistant manager, had also known the duo since the Wales under-17s and the trio had shared some of their best memories on and off the pitch together, often playing guitar and singing along together in hotels after Wales games. So Coleman and Symons were the right men to take Wales forward after Speed. After such tragic, horrific events, who better to continue your work than your best friends?

Symons reveals how keen he was to come in and work alongside the new manager. 'Chris phoned me up and told me that he'd been offered the job before it came out in the press,' says the defender who won 26 Welsh caps between 1992 and 2001. 'He asked me if I'd be interested in coming in with him and I said yes straight away. Because of the situation with Speeds, we both knew it was going to be incredibly difficult for whoever took over, but we were both mates with Gary. It was always going to be a difficult job for whoever took over, but for me and Chris it was doubly hard because we'd been such good friends for such a long time with Gary.'

At Coleman's unveiling, Jonathan Ford said the period since Speed's death had been extremely difficult for everybody. 'As CEO of the Football Association of Wales I did not expect to be announcing the name of a new manager in 2012, my second in two years. Everything was falling into place, surrounded by positivity with four wins in the last five games, and at the centre of it all was Gary. I will not deny that the search for a new manager has been a difficult process. We have explored every avenue, every possible scenario. We have taken on board the thoughts of the backroom staff, the players and the supporters. Long, detailed, sensitive discussions have taken place. This is not something we wanted to rush into, nor was it something we wanted to be pushed into. Gary Speed was the manager, the manager of Welsh football with a clear goal on qualification for a major tournament – Brazil 2014 the aim – the same aim remains today. The manager, not a figurehead, and that is why we have decided on the appointment of Chris Coleman as the manager of Welsh football.'

Ford's 'figurehead' comment was in reference to those who were calling for Raymond Verheijen and Osian Roberts to stay on to continue Speed's work with a figurehead like Ian Rush or Ryan Giggs to lead the team from the front. The FAW didn't want that and Association president Phil Pritchard, in particular, was key in pushing for Coleman to come in. There would be no place for Verheijen in Coleman's set-up.

As for Coleman himself, his performance in that conference was incredible. I can't comprehend how difficult it must have been for him – I don't think many of us could – but whether many people at the time admitted it or not, he was very impressive in that room on that day, dealing with all sorts of incredibly difficult questions. Coleman's first response demonstrated how conflicted he was. 'None of us want to be here,' he said, 'least of all me, to be honest with you. Whilst on one hand it is the proudest moment of my career to be given the opportunity to lead my country, I'm given that opportunity because of the circumstances which nobody could foresee, so it's bittersweet for me. I was very close friends with Gary for 30 years so it is a difficult experience for me, probably the most difficult press conference I've ever done or am ever going to do. I'm very proud but I'm very sad because of the situation we find ourselves in.'

Coleman was asked whether or not the results of his next few games as manager would serve to reflect on Gary Speed's legacy. He was asked how he'd overcome the perception of his managerial career being – in his own words – chequered. How would he set about getting his players on board? It wasn't easy to answer such questions but he handled himself very well. Asked by Rob Phillips to give a message to the Welsh fans, Coleman replied: 'I'm not Gary Speed. I never had a career like he had. Although we were very close friends I'm a different personality. I'm not here to disrupt anything. I'm here to try and build on the good work that he left us. I need the fans on board, the players need the fans on board. I'm not here for my ego, I'm here because it's the biggest honour and the pinnacle of my managerial career and I need the fans to be with us because I know what they can be like when they're with us. The atmosphere they create, there's nothing like it. Of course I need them to be with us because if we're all singing from the same hymn sheet then we've got half a chance, because we've got a good squad here now but we all need to be together and I need to play my part in that, which I will do.'

Wales left-back Neil Taylor remembers how impressed he was by his new manager in Coleman's first meeting with the squad. 'He was great, it must have been incredibly difficult for him to come in and speak to the lads and to take over from what was a successful team, but he didn't mind doing it,' says Taylor. 'He has that strength of character about him where it doesn't matter what people outside think or how people perceive him. He was only concerned with doing right by the players and Wales and giving it everything. He talked about the difficulty of the circumstances and said he wasn't going to come in and change things but wanted to implement his own stuff, bring in a few people and we went from there. He knew the way we were playing was pretty close to perfect, not too dissimilar to where he wanted it to be and we were already playing well. He was a motivated guy. He still is now. You can still see the passion when he's out there. If he could still play he would be out there with us and that passion was definitely felt by us from the start.'

Before Wales' new manager could get down to business and put his own stamp on the team, though, he and his players and the Welsh nation had to contend with the myriad of emotions that had overcome them since the moment they'd all heard of Speed's death. Paying tribute to Speed's memory is something that everybody had done individually in the six weeks preceding Coleman's appointment. But the chance to come together and celebrate the legacy of one of the country's sporting icons would beckon at the Cardiff City Stadium on 29 February 2012, as Wales invited Costa Rica – the team Speed made his Wales debut against – to play in the Gary Speed Memorial Match. What better way to pay tribute to the man than playing a football match with 30,000+ of his most ardent supporters singing his name, with his family and a who's who of football legends there as well? Coleman stepped away from the spotlight for this match, opting instead to let Osian Roberts – a key member of Speed's backroom staff who would become a key member of Coleman's in the years to come – manage the team for this incredible occasion.

The FAW were praised massively for the way they handled Speed's death and arranged such a perfect tribute to his memory, but Jonathan Ford recalls the immense complexity of the situation. 'I've been through an awful lot of things in my career as a senior manager and in various other roles learning about crisis management and things like that, but you may as well have pushed all of that to one side in this case, because absolutely none of it was relevant,' he says. 'What we did do? We did everything we could for his parents, showing them where he worked, lived, did things, so we had to have a lot of very careful discussions with people. What we also did is we talked. We talked very well. From personal experience, I've dealt with very close deaths and I did what I thought was right by my heart and it was our hearts that we allowed to make the decisions for us in this case. Absolutely surreal, but the nice thing about what we did, I suppose, is that people have written about it since, the way we handled it. We absolutely brought the team together. We made sure that we had time for the staff, that we were doing the right thing with the press and the media.'

Beautiful, surreal, difficult, essential, perfect – all words that have been used by people who've spoken to me about that match, a night where nobody wanted to be there because they all wanted their manager, friend, son, dad, brother, idol back. And yet everyone wanted to be there to pay their respects and remember Speed in the best way possible.

Wales lost to Costa Rica, thanks to an early goal from Joel Campbell, so the result didn't give Speed a perfect tribute from the sporting perspective, but otherwise it was flawless. From the enormous 'Gary' tifo displayed by fans in the Canton End in the colours of the Welsh flag, to all the songs sung in his memory, the plethora of former internationals who took part in an extended half-time tribute to Speed, the family being there and Speed's sons walking out with the players and singing the anthem before the match, it was as fitting a tribute as you could ever hope to give anyone.

Coleman admitted he wasn't looking forward to the occasion and that he hadn't been himself in the days leading up to it, but was particularly moved by Speed's teenage son Ed. 'Ed has come into the dressing room after the game and he gave a speech that anybody would have been proud of,' said Coleman. 'There was not a tear in his eyes. He was strong as an ox. He came in and he said, "My dad always said to me that if you do your best it's enough, and I think you lot did your best tonight." So what do you say to that, when a 14-year-old boy who's just lost his dad speaks like that to a bunch of professional footballers? What do you say to that – that's bravery, isn't it?'

Brave, inspirational, it was certainly something very special. As was the entire occasion and, although it only lasted for one night, the memories people would take from Cardiff, as well as the memories that Speed had given each and every supporter throughout his career, would never be forgotten in light of the achievements that Wales were still to accomplish in years to come.

The herculean task now began for Chris Coleman of rebuilding a nation that had suffered a most heartbreaking loss. During the latter days of Speed's managerial tenure the players, the fans and the coaches had all had a real belief that they could face anyone, anytime and beat them. A key feather in Coleman's cap was that the experienced Craig Bellamy had chosen to stay on and continue his international career under his leadership. Now in his thirties it would have been easy for Bellamy to step aside, particularly given how close he had been to Speed, so to see him stay on spoke a lot in Coleman's favour. In spite of this, everyone knew it would take time.

Everyone was ready, but few appreciated the immense psychological effects the loss of Speed would have on the players and coaching staff. Any new manager has to put their own stamp on a team, but in such delicate circumstances it must have been incredibly difficult for Coleman to know when to do that and when to just sit back and let things take their course, while trying to implement his own ideas as slowly and as sensitively as he could. 'I don't think anyone fully appreciated the difficulty of the circumstances,' says Chris Wathan of Wales Online. 'I don't think I did. Although I felt the sense of loss as everyone did, I don't think we appreciated the sense of loss the players felt every time they went back into camp. Coleman lost a great friend and was obviously battling with the turmoil of not wanting to tread on his friend's legacy and rip up things that had gone before. At the same time though you can't walk in somebody else's shoes and it was clear it wasn't a comfort for Coleman in that sense – he had a great sense of loss himself, but had to be the man to replace Speed and this only added to the difficulty of the job.'

Two friendlies took place before Wales' 2014 World Cup qualifying campaign got underway, as Coleman's men travelled to America for a friendly against Mexico, a team ranked 20th in the world at the time, compared to Wales who sat in 41st place. It was always going to be a difficult game, given that it took place at the end of May, so soon after the gruelling English domestic season had finished. The absence of key players such as Gareth Bale, Joe Ledley and Wayne Hennessey also hampered Wales in the sweltering heat of New York's MetLife Stadium. Jason Brown ended up playing between the sticks for Wales for the first time in six years, as Wales were left with very few options in goal. The keeper saw enough action in those 90 minutes to make up for the time he'd been out of the starting XI, as Mexico blitzed the Welsh goal in the first half, creating over a dozen decent chances and testing Brown on a number of occasions. It took until the end of the half for him to be beaten by Aldo de Nigris. It was the cruellest time to score. Wales had worked hard in the first half, while ultimately struggling to create anything of note before falling behind, something that would become a trend in Coleman's first few games. Wales went on to concede again with de Nigris getting his second, condemning Coleman to a 2–0 defeat in his first outing as manager.

Between Mexico in May and the next game against Bosnia in August, some of Wales' players were selected to represent Team GB in the Olympics. The pre-season had got underway and the domestic season kicked off again. There was time for everyone to continue the process of coming to terms with the incredible turmoil of the last few months in their own time. When the squad reported back for the training camp before the Bosnia game, there was a conscious effort to try and be upbeat, to try and rediscover the success Wales had found in the last few months under Speed.

It was never going to be that easy, though, as Wales were beaten comfortably by Bosnia in Llanelli. 'It was only 2–0,' recalls Osian Roberts, 'but it was a good 2–0 as Bosnia could have had a couple more. We were lethargic, we were poor, the pitch wasn't great and nor was the atmosphere. Despite everybody in camp before the game trying to be upbeat, after the game we were all sat in the dressing room with a big cloud over us. It was very difficult – I remember Craig Bellamy saying "I know it's difficult for all of you, it's difficult for me but we've got to do something to get out of this." Everyone was trying their best, but no-one could have anticipated it would take so long and be so difficult for the players, staff and undoubtedly for Chris.'

After winning four of their last five under Speed, Wales had lost all three of their games since then without scoring a single goal and some were, very unfairly, pointing the finger at the manager. The narrow-minded approach to the criticism was that only the manager had changed, therefore it must be the manager's fault that things weren't going very well. Absolute rubbish. The manager may have been the only thing that had changed, plus one or two backroom staff, but had a managerial change ever occurred under such harrowing circumstances? When the former manager had been idolised by all of his players?

Blaming Coleman for any of the lacklustre performances that materialised as a result was incredibly insensitive, if nothing else. 'It was harsh,' says Matty Jones. 'It was a difficult start for him in horrendous circumstances. For him to be criticised after a few games and for a lot of negativity to be thrown his way, I was disgusted by it. It was horrible to experience.'

It was about to get a lot more difficult for Coleman, as the games were now starting to matter. Points were on the line and this World Cup qualifying campaign, despite the circumstances, was still considered by many to be the one where Wales would reach another tournament at last. The fans saw this as a good chance, regardless of a tricky group containing Belgium, Croatia, Serbia, Scotland and Macedonia. A double-header against Belgium at home and Serbia away in Novi Sad would signal Coleman's first test in competitive fixtures, but Wales' prospects looked bleak in the days leading up to the first game as their squad was ravaged with injuries. Joe Allen, Joe Ledley, Craig Bellamy, Neil Taylor, Jack Collison, Andrew Crofts and Wayne Hennessey would all miss out through injury. To put that into context, the first-choice goalkeeper, first-choice left-back, first-choice striker, first-choice midfield pairing, a very bright prospect and a great squad player were missing.

Neil Taylor, who would be out for the season with an ankle injury, offers a glowing reference of the way he was treated by his manager during his recovery. 'I had a really good summer playing in the Olympics and was ready to go for the new season,' recalls Taylor. 'Then three games in I broke my ankle. The first person to visit me in the hospital was Chris Coleman and he told me how I was going to be fine, come back well. He talked about when he was out for a while after being in a car crash and the spinal injuries that he had to come through. I knew then the character of the man. To be one of the first people to be there to see me said a lot about him and then in the next Wales game they were wearing 'Get Well Taylz' T-shirts. These subtle touches tell you everything about how close the Wales set-up was at the time, and it has only got closer since then.'

With Joe Allen out, centre-back Ashley Williams started as a defensive-midfielder for Wales. Belgium had most of the possession in the opening exchanges but struggled to break down Coleman's side. James Collins was sent off after 26 minutes as he and Guillaume Gillet lunged for a loose ball in midfield, the Welshman catching the Belgian with his studs showing. It was an incredibly harsh red card with both players as culpable as each other, but it was just Wales' luck that Gillet would come off worse for wear and make Collins' challenge look somewhat reckless. The reshuffle after that sending off was fairly simple, as Williams dropped into centre-back instead of Collins, and Wales continued to prove stubborn in the face of Belgian pressure, until Vincent Kompany put Belgium ahead two minutes before half-time – again. Wales tried to fight their way back into the game in the second half as Belgium's dominance briefly turned to complacency, which allowed Wales fans to dream of an equaliser. Gareth Bale in particular had a great opportunity to test Courtois from a free kick, but the away side would get a second through a Jan Vertonghen free kick with ten minutes to go, condemning Wales to a third defeat in three games.

Coleman would go on to ask questions of the referee after the game, particularly concerning the dubious nature of Collins' sending off, but also about the decision to award the free kick that Vertonghen scored. But he said he was delighted with the spirit his team had shown in the game to keep their heads up. It could have been 5–0 or 6–0 the way Belgium had created chances, but Wales' stubbornness and resolve – something that would serve them well in the tough months that lay ahead – was encouraging, especially while contending with so many injuries.

In the next game against Serbia, though, all of that went out of the window. Rob Phillips, who missed that game because he was having surgery, sums up how disastrous Wales' performance was in Novi Sad. 'I don't know what was causing me more pain to be honest,' says Phillips, 'the hernia or the match.' Even the most optimistic Wales fans among us would have to admit that it was as catastrophic a game as most of us had ever seen. A 6–1 defeat? The national squad hadn't suffered a defeat that heavy since 1996, and that Nineties side was a team in transition playing against a strong Netherlands side. This was supposed to be Wales' golden generation pushing on to reach the World Cup for only the second time in their history.

This was the watershed moment, when everyone realised how much this team was still suffering from the loss of

Gary Speed and how every defeat since had added to that suffering. The players felt they were letting Speed down, letting themselves down and letting their new manager and the fans down. You couldn't even find any comfort in the stats for Wales. They only had 30 per cent possession, and had to defend 22 Serbian shots – 19 of which were on target. It was an absolute mauling.

Something had to give after this. Coleman had been as humane and as respectful as possible in trying to build on Gary Speed's work in the way he thought Speed would have done it, but now was the time for change. He had to do it entirely his way. There was no other option, and you sensed in his post-match comments to the BBC that Coleman knew what had to be done. 'To say we are disappointed is an understatement,' began Coleman. 'We have to do much better, because the goals we conceded were criminal. We have a mountain to climb, because we have not gone into half-time on level terms in any of the four games since I've been in charge. I'm embarrassed by the performance. I have to use that word. When you play for your country you have to have a bit of bite and you have to be difficult to beat. We've got the players to play football, we know that, but we have to earn the right to do that.'

If Speed and Toshack had taught this team how to play with the ball, then undoubtedly what changed, and what the legacy of Coleman would be from this game forward, was how they were going to play without it. The manager knew he had to change the playing style accordingly but you could sense, and Coleman himself has since admitted as much, that he had wanted to carry on the work of his best friend. You can imagine the conflict in him during those first five games leading up to this moment against Serbia. That might have been what was going through Coleman's head in the airport on the day after the game, as Kit Symons recalls seeing his best friend sitting on his own. 'Chris was sat there looking like the loneliest man in the world,' says Symons. 'So I went and sat with him and then we were the two loneliest men in the world. That was the time when Chris knew he had to do it completely his own way and it was after that when things started to pick up. It was such a difficult time. Because we were so close to Gary we were sensitive about the way we did things but, undoubtedly, that Serbia game is when we realised we had to start doing it Chris' way from then on.'

It was a big call for Coleman to decide to do things his own way, because what Speed was doing was working. But then you have to do things your own way as a manager. You have to go with your instincts. When Coleman changed the team captain after the Serbia game from Aaron Ramsey to Ashley Williams, there was no disputing any more that the manager was now doing things his own way. Coleman has since proved that he isn't afraid to make the big calls, with Wales playing some innovative formations in more recent times. But taking the captaincy from the player who had been the embodiment of the Gary Speed team was arguably the biggest and most important call he has made to date, possibly that he ever will make. It was a statement – he might not have won games after changing the captain, but if he didn't then at least he would have lost doing things his way, as opposed to getting closer and closer to the sack by trying to continue someone else's work.

Just as Ramsey had been the personification of Speed's ethos, Williams would be the same for Coleman. Level-headed, tactically astute and, above all, a rock-solid fighter, he has been an absolute colossus at the heart of the Wales defence ever since he made his debut, and it spoke volumes for Coleman's plans for the team going forward. Ramsey had been a good captain, but he's the sort of player who wants to do everything. An intense thinker, he would have felt more under pressure than your usual captain as the winless run grew. Giving the armband to Williams lifted the pressure of responsibility off such a young man's shoulders, and Ramsey handled the decision brilliantly, concentrating on playing his football. He's played some great football since then and with Williams scaling new heights performance-wise since accepting that extra responsibility, it turned out to be a masterstroke from Coleman.

The next game, a British derby against Scotland, was always going to be huge but in the circumstances it took on even more significance. If Wales lost, more questions would have been asked about Coleman's job security – the manager himself confessed to being weary of the results that the side had accumulated. But with a new captain came a new sense of optimism. In the build-up to the game Ashley Williams explained how the squad tried to take the pressure off Coleman. 'We feel like we kind of let him down a little bit on the pitch to be honest,' said Williams. 'We really want to win the game for him because we know he is under a little bit of pressure. He has come under criticism... but we feel it's a little bit unfair because it's not really his fault, it's more ours. Everyone is really happy with him and I can speak for the rest of the lads, we need to win the game for him as well as ourselves and the country.'

Ben Davies of Swansea City was given his Wales debut in this fixture, someone who would become a big part of the Welsh defence in years to come. In a typically scrappy derby game, Scotland took the lead with a goal from James Morrison after 27 minutes, sandwiched by two great chances for Wales that Gareth Bale had put on a plate for Steve Morrison and Aaron Ramsey. Yet again it seemed like Wales weren't going to get the luck, as Scotland were in unusually vibrant form in the first half with their attacking play.

The second half told a different story and would drastically change the course of Chris Coleman's managerial career with Wales, with elements of the performance in that 45 minutes becoming a prominent feature in Coleman's Wales team right up to the moment it qualified for France. Wales' comeback in this one was special; it was pantomime stuff. Under heavy rain and with a vociferous crowd wanting to see Coleman's side push on after a difficult start to his tenure, the atmosphere inside Cardiff City Stadium was, as BBC Sport's Thomas McGuigan noted, 'off the emotional scale'. A second goal for Scotland was ruled out after an out-swinging cross headed in by Steven Fletcher was dubiously adjudged to have gone out of play on its way into the six-yard box. This gave Wales the initiative and Gareth Bale, who had been an absolute nightmare for Scotland throughout the game, went on to win and convert a crucial penalty with ten minutes to go. The scores were level.

What happened next was absolutely sublime, with Bale scoring what should go down as one of the most important goals in his career. Picking up the ball near the halfway line, Bale burned through the Scottish midfield, brushed off the tight marking of Charlie Adam and launched a rocket into the far corner of Alan McGregor's goal from 25 yards to give Wales a 2–1 lead with hardly any time at all left to go in the game. It was a stunning goal and Bale went berserk in celebration, as did the Wales bench and the crowd.

It was the first time Wales had been able to celebrate anything at all in a whole year, after suffering nothing but misery since the loss of their former manager. Coleman's emotional reaction from the bench was matched by his players. Watching footage of that winning goal now on YouTube, and the celebrations that followed, it is clear that there was something more to it than it simply just being a great goal. It was the first step in a long road to Wales finding that belief again. Backs against the wall, Wales had kept plugging away. They'd got a bit of luck and showed real collective spirit to push through, before a bit of individual brilliance decided the game for them.

'The Gareth Bale goal was just immense,' recalls Jonathan Ford, who saw it from the director's box. 'The whole match was quite special and it really was such an amazing comeback, a beautiful goal too, just stunning. We all went ballistic in celebration. Serbia was a big wake-up call, a massive one. The good thing in this job is that you don't need to turn around to a player or a manager and say "That was poor" because they know, and you would expect professionals of that ilk to be able to sit down, to assess what worked and what didn't and to come to you with a plan. We didn't sit Chris down and tell him that, he knew. The players also probably had a good look at themselves and thought "We can do this. We can make this work. We don't want to play in front of 10,000 people, we want to play in front of sell-out crowds. We want to go to major tournaments and play at the highest level," and I think after Serbia it was a reality check for everyone. And Chris, to his credit, has very much led all of that change.'

Results would improve for Coleman from this point onwards with Wales winning two, drawing one and losing two of their next five. Wins in the friendly against Austria and the reverse qualifying fixture against Scotland in Hampden Park, where Jonny Williams made his international debut in midfield replacing Gareth Bale, would prove great indicators of Coleman's progress. But there was still a lot of work to do. Osian Roberts describes how that second Scotland game, where Wales again went behind before coming back to win 2–1, was the perfect example of why Wales had to improve defensively. 'Our work has been about adding a dimension of being very solid, being very compact and being able to play as a good counterattacking team,' he says. 'We've worked hard on having more than one answer, because we've been one-dimensional at times. For example, we go to Scotland and play them off the park, probably the best football we've played since I've been involved, and yet we go in at half-time 1–0 down. So that's the point really – we want to play good football, but we don't want to be soft to play against and concede easily and the players have taken that on board and see the value of our work. Then it's a case of setting targets and goals for each game.'

With ten games as Wales manager already under Coleman's belt, and his side winning three and drawing one of those fixtures, the pressure was very much on with the end of their World Cup 2014 qualification campaign approaching in September and October and Coleman's contract expiring a month after that. There were four games left for Coleman to end the campaign on an encouraging note: Macedonia away, Serbia at home, Macedonia at home and Belgium away. With talisman Gareth Bale completing his world-record move to Real Madrid, and Aaron Ramsey having started the season for Arsenal in incredible form, Wales had a great chance to capitalise on the extra attention that was being directed their way.

Coleman stoked the fire by saying he wanted his side to get six points from its next two games to aid Wales' hopes of finishing third in their group. Before the first game, however, he misplaced his passport and missed the flight out with his team, having to join up with them later that day, and this, somewhat unfairly, drew a fair amount of negative press his way. On top of this, his side couldn't turn their good play against Macedonia into a result, losing 2–1 without the injured Bale. Coleman would say after that first Macedonia game that what he felt was missing was the ability to 'stick the knife' into other teams when Wales were blatantly on top, as they had been throughout most of the game. Despite the obvious improvements defensively, Wales' lack of a clinical touch in front of goal was killing them.

In the next game against Serbia, where a plethora of injuries hampered Wales again – Ashley Williams, Joe Allen, Jonny Williams and Sam Ricketts were among those who missed out – even those defensive improvements that Wales had made over the last few games went awry. Serbia picked up where they'd left off in Novi Sad and won 3–0 without suffering too much resistance from the Welsh. Chants of 'We Want Coleman Out' could be heard from sections of the Welsh fans inside the stadium, as the manager's days looked well and truly numbered. However, FAW president Trefor Lloyd Hughes gave Coleman a vote of confidence the day after the game, saying that he hadn't yet had an opportunity to prove himself properly.

Going into the home game against Macedonia, Coleman acknowledged that his future was on the line as Wales were bottom of their group, with very slim hopes of reaching third and boosting their seeding for the next qualification campaign. A new deal for the manager had been agreed in principle, but neither Coleman nor his employers had signed it, so that told its own story really. Of all the teams and situations Wales had faced in Coleman's tenure, this on paper should have been the least significant. This was the lowest ranked team they'd faced, playing at home with nothing but pride on the line. Under the circumstances, however, it seemed exactly the opposite. Ten Welsh players missed out again through injury, including key players such as captain Ashley Williams, Joe Allen, Gareth Bale, Joe Ledley and Ben Davies.

Joe Ledley and Joe Allen – labelled the 'Joe-Axis' – had been crucial to the spine of the team because of the way they controlled and distributed possession of the ball. To have these two missing more often than not in Coleman's tenure up to this point was a crucial factor in why his side had struggled to get results. Neil Taylor, who returned in this game more than a year after his last appearance for Wales, sums up the importance of their dual role. 'Joe Ledley and Joe Allen have done so well,' he says. 'That position is one of the most difficult you can play in, because you're guaranteed to come up against the opposition's best players there, you've got to know what's around you constantly, and they've done brilliantly to break up and start plays. They show real bravery to get on the ball too and help Wales play a certain style of football that maybe hasn't been played down the years. The centre-midfielders have been crucial for that and the control they've given us has been key.'

Forced to chop and change their line-up against Macedonia, Wales were made to work hard early on, but soon found some joy down the flanks with the livewire Hal Robson-Kanu, someone who would become a cult hero for Wales fans in years to come, having a couple of penalty shouts turned down. Wales were caught napping at the back once or twice as Macedonia missed a chance at an open goal before half-time. But in the second half Aaron Ramsey, stepping back in as captain in Williams' absence, took the game by the scruff of the neck.

Wales worked their socks off, pushed themselves hard and finally got the lead through Simon Church with 20 minutes to go. In front of one of the smallest crowds to watch Wales in recent times, 'Churchy' had just scored the goal that his manager admitted after the match would save his job. Wales could have had another had Ramsey's late penalty not been saved, but Coleman was delighted as he spoke to the BBC. 'Had we lost this game I would have been out the door,' he said. 'Looking at our squad of players and all the pull-outs we had, I am delighted. I enjoyed the win tonight more than any other because there has been a lot said and we were up against it. The players stood up to the test.'

Wales' biggest test under Coleman up to this point was still to come, though – facing Belgium, in Brussels. The pretext to this game was that it was just going to be a big Belgian party; they'd qualified for the World Cup for the first time in 12 years, going unbeaten in the group with eight wins and a draw, and were many pundits' outside bet to win the World Cup the next summer in Brazil. Wales would have reason to start their own parties when facing the Belgians in years to come, but on this night it was the home fans who were celebrating like lunatics. Mexican waves, raves, the Belgians were just going crazy, and they belted out their anthem so passionately that I've only seen the Welsh and the Brazilians rival it since. Belgium clearly expected this game to be a walkover, to wipe the floor with the Welsh and sail into Brazil on a high, but it didn't quite happen like that. The Welsh support did their best to match them in terms of volume and didn't stop singing all night as their team – still without Bale, Williams, Ledley and Allen – played very well against a weakened Belgium team that had big names like Eden Hazard and Christian Benteke warming the bench.

Wales were outdone in terms of possession and had to weather a lot of opposition pressure, but there was a lot of encouragement to be taken from the performance of Coleman's men in this game. They went into half-time with the scores level at 0–0 thanks to some unbelievable Wayne Hennessey saves, while Craig Bellamy, making his last ever appearance for Wales, and the rest of the team ran themselves ragged to keep Belgium at bay. When Hazard entered the fray just before the hour mark, Belgium cranked everything up a gear and went for the jugular, going ahead six minutes later through Kevin De Bruyne. Everyone expected the floodgates to open now. Belgium's fans, flares in hands, upped the ante inside the stadium, but Wales stayed defiant, hoping their immense effort and perseverance would pay off. Just as it looked like Coleman's men would go home with a respectable 1–0 defeat, Bellamy's final significant act in a Wales shirt was to set-up an unbelievable equaliser. The 34 year old drifted out wide, dragging two defenders with him, and played a beautiful ball into the path of Aaron Ramsey who, cutting into the box, placed his shot low between the legs of Thibaut Courtois from an impossible angle. Wales had a fully deserved, incredible equaliser with just two minutes to go.

Suddenly everything was forgotten. Every struggle that Wales had gone through in the last 18 months under Coleman was gone and everyone was revelling in this incredible moment. Wales had gone to Brussels without some of their best players, played one of the best teams in the world and grabbed an incredible point. The party after that game carried on long into the early hours of the morning in Belgium and the memories of that success and that experience would fuel the team going forward. 'Belgium away where we got that draw with an unrecognisable team was a big one,' recalls Neil Taylor. 'We played really, really well, got the result and we started to realise how much strength in depth we had. If you can do it against Belgium in Brussels you can do it against anyone, and that result really helped us going forward.'

Wales and Coleman never looked back from that point onwards, as the manager would sign a new contract until the end of the next campaign and his team would reel off good results against Finland and Iceland. Wales lost 2–0 to the Dutch in what was a pre-World Cup friendly for the latter team, but in that run of games Coleman gave debuts to promising young players like Emyr Huws and George Williams. Wales showed real promise against Holland, as Coleman used the game to give youngsters a chance, particularly a new recruit who would add a lot to Wales on the defensive end of the pitch. James Chester of Hull City proved a revelation at the heart of the Wales defence in the qualifying campaign to come. Warrington-born Chester could have opted to play for England but was won over by Coleman. 'What was important for me was Chris Coleman ringing me and wanting me to come down and play,' says the defender. 'I was obviously aware of the increase in performances around that time and to have world-class players in the squad like Aaron and Gareth is something else I was aware of. I'd heard that everyone enjoyed playing for Chris Coleman and since I've become involved I've found that to be the case for myself as well.' There were other positives for Wales to take from this game. Although Reading had told Wales that their defender Chris Gunter was unable to take part in the friendly due to injury, Gunter himself had phoned up Coleman after the squad was announced and said he was ready and very keen to play. On the night he joined in a back four with new recruit Chester, Danny Gabbidon and Neil Taylor, as Bale, Ramsey and Ashley Williams missed out again.

This was a big test and a big performance for Wales ahead of the qualification campaign that was to come. The fixture would later be hailed as the catalyst for Wales' future success. Their improvements were being noticed. They had lost only one of their last five matches. Players were exceptionally keen to turn up and be involved, and even keener to play under Coleman. After an incredibly difficult first two years as Wales manager, he, his players and his staff had turned it all around and their chance to make history and qualify for only their second major tournament would beckon in the months ahead.

CHAPTER 8

Andorra vs Wales – 9 September 2014

'We went into this campaign with real optimism,
but when we went 1–0 down after six minutes I felt like
walking out and flying home to be honest!'

AIDEN WILLIAMS, WALES FAN

OVER THE YEARS, mostly thanks to their seeding, Wales haven't been blessed with the luck of the draw. In the last two World Cup qualifying groups, for example, they were paired with Belgium and Croatia in 2014 and Germany and Russia in 2010. Their recent European qualification groups have featured Belgium, the Czech Republic and Germany. Not exactly pretty reading. But this didn't stop the majority of supporters being full of optimism when the time came for the draw. Though one supporter told me that he just wanted 'to see if we could get any nice away days', this sort of pessimism has been limited to a minority of fans and quickly faded away when Wales has began to strut their stuff in this campaign.

The draw for the Euro '16 qualification campaign was made in February 2014 and Chris Coleman's side drew Andorra, Cyprus, Israel and two of Europe's recent World Cup finalists – Bosnia & Herzegovina and, yet again, Belgium. The schedule played into Wales' hands – an opening game away to Andorra in September, the lowest seed in the group, followed by two home games in October against Bosnia and Cyprus would set the side up perfectly to face one of the most exciting teams in the world, and the group's second seed, Belgium away from home in November.

On top of that, the qualification format had changed for

this most recent UEFA tournament, as the quota for the final tournament was expanded from 16 teams to 24. This meant that each of the nine groups' top two teams, and the best third-placed team, would qualify automatically for the finals and the other third-placed teams would get a play-off spot. Having won two, drawn two and lost just one of their last five matches, Wales' form going into the group meant that fans were optimistic of the side's chances of getting at least a play-off spot. With a depth in the squad that Wales had probably never had before, very good players in every position, a bit of luck with the fixtures and other factors coming to Wales' aid, there was a real optimism that this campaign could go well right from the start.

Those who had been involved with the Wales set-up for a while, however, were much more reserved in their optimism early on. 'Nobody knows in the game of football,' said FAW president at the time, Trefor Lloyd Hughes. 'Who would have thought that Paul Bodin would have missed that penalty against Romania back in 1993? I think that we have a good team and we've got a good chance of qualifying, yes, but the support is crucial.'

The Welsh away support has always been incredible, but in this qualifying campaign Wales more or less filled their allocation for every single game. Andorra were very generous in their allocation of tickets, too, as UEFA regulations say that home teams are only required to give a five per cent allocation of tickets to away teams. In the case of Andorra's 3,300-seat stadium, this would have resulted in just 165 tickets for Wales fans, but Andorra instead gave a 37 per cent allocation of 1,200 tickets. That was half of what Wales would be given in Belgium two months later in a 50,000-seat stadium, so it was a great gesture by the Andorran FA. Wales fans went over to Andorra in their droves to watch the opening game of what everybody was adamant would be a historic campaign. The support from Wales fans was absolutely incredible; every single one of them had been through hell and back with their team, so they didn't waste their many opportunities to celebrate as this campaign rolled on.

But despite the optimism, Wales still had problems to deal with from the start. In Andorra, the problem was quite a big one – the pitch. Wales were made aware, before the World Cup started in Brazil the previous June, that they'd be playing on a 3G pitch for their game in Andorra, and that was a controversial decision in itself. Should teams be playing on 3G pitches in qualification games for one of the world's biggest football tournaments? Arguably not. After announcing a week previously that last-minute work needed to be done on the playing surface to make it playable, on 2 September, a week before the game was due to take place, UEFA undertook a very late pitch inspection. The pitch passed the inspection, but the late work done on it did not bode well, though the Welsh chose to play this down.

Within the Wales squad there were a number of players who had extensive experience working with 3G pitches, but even those players were struggling to deal with Andorra's pitch. 'The pitch hadn't settled,' says Osian Roberts. 'They shouldn't have played on it really. The ball was bouncing all over the place; sometimes with top-spin, sometimes with back-spin. The Swansea lads who are used to 3G (they'd played for over a season on 3G pitches whilst their new training ground was being built) were even struggling with it.' Much of the pre-match media attention focused on the pitch, but also brought attention to the fact that this was a great opportunity for Wales to get their qualifying campaign off to the perfect start against a team who had failed to win in their last 40 European qualifiers, failing to score competitively for four years.

The Welsh starting line-up in Andorra was an unfamiliar one to supporters. Coleman and Roberts opted to go for a 3–5–2 formation, playing with three centre-backs and wing-backs in order to develop some familiarity with the system that the management had decided they wanted to use for the upcoming Bosnia game. Hennessey started in goal with Chester, Ashley

Williams and Ben Davies as centre-backs and Neil Taylor and Chris Gunter as wing-backs. Andy King, Joe Allen and Aaron Ramsey played in the middle as Bale and Simon Church started up front.

There was a big sense of anticipation ahead of the game given the number of supporters that had travelled out, not just the 1,200 who had tickets but the rest who had just come along for the experience. One supporter in particular told me of his experiences as an 'away day traveller' over the last few years: 'The minute the draw came out with Andorra it was a no-brainer to go there. I'd never seen Wales win away before and really thought we'd do it this time – I'd been to see us in Serbia where we got thumped 6–1, and in Macedonia when we lost 2–1 too, so I thought this was the chance to break that hoodoo.' This sentiment was echoed by many, as a lot of supporters were quietly confident that this campaign could be the start of something special.

That optimism was dented quite soon after kick-off. Talk of the pitch being of a questionable standard was an understatement to say the least – every single attempted pass of the ball resulted in plumes of black rubber marbles flying up from the pitch, disrupting the movement of the ball and seriously affecting both sets of players' judgment. It had to be seen to be believed – it was awful. You see a bit of residue popping up from most 3G pitches when there are passes zipping across it, but this was unlike anything most of those in attendance had ever seen before. It looked as if the players were kicking beehives, not footballs. The way the pitch stifled the pace of the ball was particularly detrimental to the Welsh effort, with their philosophy being to build their play from the back using quick, intricate, one- or two-touch passing sequences in the middle of the park, either to cut through the middle of teams or spread the play wide, where Wales use the natural pace of their wingers to get crosses or cut-backs and create good goal-scoring opportunities.

To make matters worse, after just six minutes Wales went

1–0 down in a controversial manner. After failing to clear from a long throw by Andorra, Neil Taylor was penalised by the assistant behind the goal who thought the wing-back had pulled the shirt of Ivan Lorenzo. The referee initially waved it away but his assistant protested, causing the referee to change his mind and award the penalty, giving Andorra a great chance to score their first competitive goal in four years. Their centre-back and captain, Lima, stepped up to take the penalty and sent Wayne Hennessey the wrong way to give Andorra, with all due respect, a very unexpected lead very early on. There was a strong feeling among Welsh fans I spoke to of 'same old Wales', 'here we go again', and 'always doing it the hard way'. Some fans even expressed a desire to head straight to the airport and fly home.

'When we went 1–0 down I was fuming,' recalls Hennessey. 'I really wanted the clean sheet as much as anyone. It was just one of those games. It was a terrible pitch. We had a day before the game to try it out and all that – Bale and all of the other lads were taking shots at me and the ball was just bouncing off the floor and over me. It was just like the standard 3G you'd get in a school – it was shocking.'

Getting the win looked even more unlikely now, as Andorra were happy to park in their own half, with Wales struggling to break them down. Though many had been unsure about Coleman's 3–5–2 formation when the line-ups had been announced, it was that width that got Wales back into the game as Ben Davies advanced from his defensive position to deliver a very inviting early cross into the box for the onrushing Gareth Bale, who nodded the ball inside the far post for the equaliser midway through the first half. With a large amount of possession, Wales were in a prime position to grab the lead before half-time but struggled to get going properly because of the pitch, and the Welsh went in at half-time with a number of fans booing what they'd just witnessed.

During the interval the Welsh coaching team had a job to do. 'Players were coming off saying they couldn't move the ball quickly enough,' says Osian Roberts. 'They couldn't run with the ball, couldn't play any one-touch football, so it was a difficult night. But we just had to tell them to stick with it because we were confident that the way we were playing would get the result.'

The confidence of the management was eventually repaid as Wales' influence on proceedings grew throughout the second half – by the end of the game Wales would amass 76 per cent possession. Nevertheless, chance after chance went begging until the game entered the last ten minutes and the world's most expensive player stepped up to grab his and Wales' second goal with an absolutely wonderful free kick. It was one of those amazing strikes that you just knew was in when he hit it. Bale has often left fans, players, coaches – anyone interested in football – dumbfounded by his talents, and on this occasion he had sent the travelling fans into absolute delirium to boot.

One travelling supporter described the atmosphere inside the stadium: 'The only time I think you'll see Wales fans celebrating more than they did for that goal would be if we won the World Cup!' It was just an exceptional effort, and an incredibly important goal. It had taken a lot of mental strength to score as well, given the fact that the referee had been unhappy with the wall's positioning for Bale's first attempt and made him retake it. To be able to step up and take it again, not least to lash it into the back of the net like he did, showed remarkable composure.

Coleman was naturally full of praise for Bale after the game, telling the press: 'There are only two players in the world, Lionel Messi and Gareth Bale, who could have done something like that. Time's ticking, the pressure is on and wallop, it's 2–1 – Gareth was absolutely magnificent.'

The same praise wasn't being lavished on Coleman, as many fans took to social media to voice their displeasure at the performance. Wales had been minutes away from giving Andorra their first ever point in European Championship qualifying. The criticism was unfair, the pitch had been diabolical and the fact that Andorra had been expected to just roll over was ill-judged, as they were always going to be very difficult to break down. 'It was actually a really difficult game,' admits James Chester. 'We knew of their record, everyone does, but playing them at the start of the campaign wasn't as easy as it might have seemed, because they'd have been coming in with some confidence and belief. It was a difficult start, but to come away with the three points was the main thing to get us off to the right start.'

Gareth Bale's goals had won the game and everyone looked relieved – at the very least, Wales had got the job done despite the pitch. Aaron Ramsey had turned his ankle during the game and suffered for a few days with an injury, but most of the other players came away unharmed. Kit Symons lauded the fact that Wales had finally got some luck. 'The defining moment of that game is the referee taking Gareth back to take the free kick again,' he said. 'If that hadn't have gone in then we'd be looking at a very different campaign now without a doubt. We had an awful lot of bad luck in previous campaigns, so if anyone deserved some it was us and we finally got some which has hopefully set us up.'

Osian Roberts also emphasises the importance of the result in the face of such adversity. 'It was the best thing that could have happened,' he says. 'It was a proper test and we had to believe in what we were doing, keep doing what we were doing and not panic. On top of that, we'd tried a new system which we'd worked on for ten days, one we thought would be beneficial for the next game against Bosnia. So it was very testing.'

All in all, Wales had done what they had needed to do and after one game shared the lead of the group with Cyprus. The Cypriots had secured a surprise 2–1 win away at Bosnia with Israel's game with Belgium being pushed back until March as a result of the political situation in Israel at the time.

Two games at home against Bosnia and Cyprus would follow in a month's time, but for now Wales had gained some much needed practice in learning to deal with the adversity that would dog them throughout the next few games.

Standings after Matchday 1

Pos.	Team	GP	W	D	L	F	A	GD	Pts
1	Cyprus	1	1	0	0	2	1	1	3
2	Wales	1	1	0	0	2	1	1	3
3	Belgium	0	0	0	0	0	0	0	0
4	Israel	0	0	0	0	0	0	0	0
5	Andorra	1	0	0	1	1	2	- 1	0
6	Bosnia	1	0	0	1	1	2	- 1	0

Results:

Andorra 1–2 Wales

Bosnia & Herzegovina 1–2 Cyprus

Israel vs Belgium – Postponed

CHAPTER 9

Wales vs Bosnia / Wales vs Cyprus – 10 / 13 October 2014

'These are exactly the type of games we would
have lost a few years ago. Backs against the wall, this is
where we would have dropped points before, but we
showed how far we've come.'

GARY PRITCHARD, S4C's *SGORIO*

MANAGING EXPECTATIONS IS a key thing in football. As
mentioned previously, this Euro 2016 qualifying campaign was
seen as the one where Wales would have their best chance in a
long time of breaking their hoodoo and reaching the finals of
a major tournament. Taking into account the draw, the squad,
the run of fixtures, it all seemed to fall into place but, after the
Andorra game, fans were divided. Most were totally satisfied
with the result in Andorra – a character-building win to start
the group – but a minority weren't content and had wanted
more from the performance. However James Chester got it
right when he said that to have expected Andorra to just roll
over in that game was ill-advised, and Wales did well to come
through that test in such circumstances.

Building belief in and around the team was something
outlined in the 2012 FAW strategy we looked at earlier, and
these games, the first home fixtures of the campaign, were
the first chance the FAW had to capitalise on the overall
positivity that fans were showing towards the side's prospects.
It was an opportunity they didn't waste. The FAW would later
receive award nominations as a result of the success of their

Together Stronger marketing campaign – a campaign they had been working on since just after the qualifying draw back in February – and the campaign's potential really became evident in the build up to this international window. It was always going to resonate with the fans, because we all feel like we've been on this journey with the players and that we're stronger for it, but also because it's a play on the message on our badge *Gorau Chwarae, Cyd Chwarae* (The Best Play Is Team Play). The goal with the Together Stronger campaign was to make that phrase relevant to everyone who wore that badge, not just the players that wore it on the pitch, the fans in the stands, the staff, the fans who couldn't get tickets – everyone.

In the days building up to the match against Bosnia, there was the usual material on the FAW's social media pages – exclusive interviews with the players – but there was a distinct purpose to the content. The video taglines included references to doing it for the fans, having such great fans, and so on. It was clear the FAW was working hard to send out a positive message to get the fans going and excited for the game. Also, in the run-up to this game the FAW was pushing offers on tournament tickets – £75 for the five home games for adults, and £25 for kids – and running a competition to be part of a Together Stronger fan mosaic that would feature in the programme for the two matches. The Association wanted the Cardiff City Stadium absolutely rocking in time for the game. Those behind the scenes at the FAW who were involved with implementing and planning the Together Stronger campaign have told me they expected the campaign to have some sort of impact, but nothing like the impact it ended up having later in the campaign. The fans bought into it immediately, which in turn resulted in the players embracing it and then using that to fuel their own performances on the pitch, and it all really took off during this international window. Record-breaking attendances, hospitality packages selling out, a huge increase in social media presence and ticket sales – everything went through the roof once the Together Stronger campaign got going.

No matter how much positivity and belief a clever marketing campaign can generate, though, it can't protect a team from injuries, and Wales' squad was absolutely ravaged in the build up to this international window. Ten players pulled out with various injuries, but Wales were left particularly short in midfield as Aaron Ramsey missed out, along with the 'Welsh Xavi', Joe Allen – certain starters had they been fit – Emyr Huws (who would miss the majority of the campaign through injury) and David Vaughan, both very impressive players, among others. Despite the injuries, it didn't stop Chris Coleman reminding the players of what was expected of them in this campaign. Ever since Welsh fans got a whiff of the talents of Gareth Bale, Aaron Ramsey, Joe Ledley, et al. they'd been expecting a lot of this group, and their manager made it clear to them that he believed this campaign was their chance to live up to expectations.

Coleman told the media before the game how he wanted the players to learn from his experience as part of a 1994 squad that had had huge potential to do something special. 'It's awful when you're part of an international outfit that gets so close and you don't do it,' said Coleman. 'I don't want that again; I want to be part of a team that does something no-one else has. They have a great chance to live up to the tag they have been given as the golden generation.'

He also called the prospect of facing Bosnia a titanic challenge. It would have been anyway given that this was opposition that had recently been involved at the World Cup, but the injuries certainly exacerbated the scale of the challenge. In truth, though, Wales' injuries showed how far the squad had come in such a short space of time, because if Wales had lost ten players to injury in the Toshack days then he'd have had difficulty picking a high-calibre squad. The starting XI for Wales in the Bosnia game, however, included eight Premier League players. Only Simon Church, Jonny Williams and Chris

Gunter didn't have that privilege, though Gunter had over 50 caps at that point, Williams was a very exciting youth prospect and Church was fairly experienced at international level too. Jonny Williams, Andy King and Joe Ledley filled the midfield places, with Gareth Bale and Simon Church up front. Chris Gunter, James Chester, Ashley Williams, Ben Davies and Neil Taylor filled the defensive positions, with Taylor and Gunter playing as wing-backs.

Regardless of the injuries, Wales' 3–5–2 game plan was unchanged. 'We knew Bosnia were going to play with two up-front, and two good players up-front at that, and a diamond in the middle,' explains Osian Roberts. 'We had to change things the way we did by releasing a man from the back to put more players in the central area, or we'd have had to revert to man-marking which we didn't want to do. To make the switch was a positive thing, because we'd watched Bosnia against other teams and the way they play gives them advantages in areas of the pitch that most teams just can't deal with.'

One of the highlights of this campaign was to see Osian Roberts get the recognition he deserved – he's excellent, exceptionally knowledgeable, and if you ever see him and talk tactics with him then I promise you, whoever you are, you'll learn a few things about football. Some of the Welsh-language media told me they noticed he was getting more popular during the course of the campaign, as they used to be the only ones who regularly interviewed Roberts for their shows, since he's a Welsh speaker, but as this campaign progressed everyone wanted to interview him.

Bosnia's manager was talking tactics in his press conference too. He was adamant that he didn't have a specific plan to stop Gareth Bale and that there wouldn't be any man-marking involved to slow him down. Needless to say, he was lying.

The Bosnia game was Wales' first home game in seven months – an incredibly long time but understandable given the World Cup tournament over that summer – but the support took the atmosphere to an entirely new level in this game.

Cardiff City Stadium was a 30,000+ sell-out. To put that into context, the last three attendances for Wales games there had peaked at 13,000. The excitement around the place was absolutely immense. Wales captain Ashley Williams had said in his pre-match press conference how much he was relishing the occasion. 'I've never played for Wales in front of a full house before,' he said. 'Having all of that noise behind you can really help you in the last minutes of the game when you need that extra 5 per cent. I really can't wait to walk out and see all of our fans there.' After the game Wayne Hennessey, who had sampled the home support in many games since his debut in 2007, would say the support against Bosnia had been the loudest he'd ever heard.

The away following was equally vociferous. Some Bosnia fans had even managed to get tickets for the home end, which shows how desperate they were to be involved in the game. All in all, every one of the 30,741 people inside the stadium made an immense contribution to the spectacle of the game.

The match itself wasn't a classic by any means, but it was a very gutsy performance from Wales as Bosnia bossed the possession. All talk of there being no specific Bosnian plan to limit Gareth Bale's effectiveness was dismissed immediately as Muhamed Bešić, Bosnia's holding midfielder, was practically an arm's length away from Bale throughout the game. The first chance of the match fell to Wales, as Ashley Williams headed over the bar from a Jonny Williams corner, before Miralem Pjanić went down the other end minutes later and got what would be the first of many shots on target to test Wayne Hennessey.

These two proved to be a thorn in each other's side throughout the night, as Bosnia had eight shots on target and it seemed like all of them either came from Pjanić or he was heavily involved in the build-up for each effort. But Hennessey looked very solid and pulled off some spectacular saves to keep the Bosnians at bay. Bale and Gunter both went close for Wales before the 20-minute mark, but after that it was pretty much the Pjanić show in the first half as he was in imperious form. Wales did really well in holding their defensive shape and dealing with Bosnia's other key players like Edin Džeko and Vedad Ibišević – both were anonymous, thanks to Wales' defensive efforts – but Pjanić gave them a lot to think about. The Roma star has been hailed, by Craig Bellamy in particular, as Barcelona or Real Madrid quality and he demonstrated that throughout this game. But he still couldn't beat the excellent Hennessey in goal.

If the opening 45 minutes had been a bit scrappy from both teams – a lot of tedious fouls, a few misplaced passes – the second period saw some much better football being played. Bale and Ashley Williams had good chances to put Wales ahead early on, but Jonny Williams and Joe Ledley were the real driving force for Wales in midfield – the former showing the kind of form that saw him reel off man-of-the-match performances at youth level for club and country and the latter showing real resolve and toughness to break up a lot of the Bosnian play. Williams was at the forefront of a lot of Wales' good offensive work, running time and again at the opposition and forcing them into mistakes, an incredible display since he hadn't been playing regularly at senior domestic level.

Wales' fortunes further improved towards the end of the game as fresh legs added new impetus to the attack, with an increased emphasis on running at the opposition. Wales created a number of chances as a result that could have given them a comfortable win, with Hal Robson-Kanu entering the fray on 65 minutes for Jonny Williams and George Williams coming on in the last ten minutes for Simon Church. The most striking thing about the closing stages of the game was Gareth Bale; not because of what he was doing with the ball at his feet, but for something else: his passion. We all know how passionate all of the players, not least Bale, are about Wales and how much they love the fans. It couldn't be more obvious. But towards the end of the Bosnia game, when the ball was firmly in Wales' court and there were a few set pieces for the Welsh to capitalise on, Bale was running to take the set pieces, repeatedly gesturing to the crowd for more support. It was inspiring to see, and the crowd responded in kind.

The Real Madrid star capped off his show of passion by creating three great goal-scoring opportunities. On the first occasion, after being fed by Neil Taylor, his shot went straight at Asmir Begović in the Bosnia goal. The second was a trademark Gareth Bale effort, coming into the final third from the left and unleashing a shot from a tight angle towards the far post, forcing Begović to tip the ball around the post. The resulting corner was also taken by Bale, one last chance to make an impact, and he supplied a great delivery into the box for his teammates – but the cross could only be headed wide from very close range and the game ended 0–0.

Wales were up against it at times facing Bosnia, and did very well to hold out the man possessed, Miralem Pjanić, but Coleman's men came alive when it mattered thanks to their talisman and some shrewd substitutions. They couldn't grab the winner, but in the circumstances at the time, playing with a squad blighted by injury against a World Cup team, many were rightly very happy with the result. Joe Ledley wasn't though. 'We were a little bit disappointed,' said Ledley. 'At home we should be getting the three points. The main thing was to build up a string of positive results and we did that by getting that point. It could have been three of course, but that point could be crucial come October.'

Chris Coleman was more buoyant than his midfield general, though. 'It was a good point, a great performance,' he said. 'We had to ride our luck a little bit because they are a good team and we knew they'd set about us early. We tried to take control of the game from the kick-off and let them know they were in a game but you know, against teams like that, you're going to have to ride your luck because they have enough quality to hurt anyone. So we had to stand up to the challenge and we did that. They've hit us, we've hit them. It was a good old-fashioned international match and we couldn't have given any more.'

Wales didn't play their best football in this game, as Coleman also confessed after the match, but they'd stuck to a game plan and got the point they needed. 'There are games against opposition we play where we won't have 60 per cent of the ball,' said Osian Roberts, 'so when we play those teams we're going to have to be comfortable in defending, and enjoy defending too, and we've had to work on that. When we can, we certainly don't want to be anything other than a good passing team – that doesn't change.'

Of course, the hard-earned point against Bosnia would seem less significant if Wales couldn't get the win in their next home game against Cyprus. Coleman confirmed, with a rueful grin, that Wales had suffered an injury to one of their best performers against Bosnia, Jonny Williams. Like Emyr Huws, Williams would miss most of the campaign through injury.

Bare bones was the term Coleman used before the Cyprus game to describe what they had to utilise in what the manager described as a potentially harder game than the one they'd played against Bosnia. For the Cyprus game Wales went back to a more conventional system, with Hennessey in goal again, and Gunter, Chester, Williams and Taylor lining the back four. Hal Robson-Kanu and George Williams were rewarded with starting slots on the wings after their impressive performances against Bosnia, while King and Ledley occupied the centre of midfield again with Church leading the line and Bale playing just behind him.

Another stunning atmosphere welcomed the players on to the pitch, but Church left the match after just six minutes with a shoulder injury. The entire Welsh faithful seemed to hold its breath when Bale was the victim of a cynical challenge by Marios Nicolaou in the early exchanges – physicality would very much become a feature of Cyprus' play in this fixture – but thanks to early substitute David Cotterill, Wales soon kicked on. Bale had a couple of good efforts denied in the opening ten minutes before Birmingham City winger David Rhys George Best Cotterill, to give him his full name, scored a goal that Best himself might have been proud of, sending a cross into the box which evaded everyone and bounced into the goal. There was obviously an element of luck about the way with which Cotterill had given his team the lead, but when your team, at this point, has been the victim of 12 injuries in an international window, I don't think anyone could begrudge Wales a bit of luck.

Chris Coleman's men soon doubled their lead, with Bale involved again as he sent a sublime back-heeled pass into the path of Robson-Kanu, who had got a run on the Cyprus defence and was in on goal. He slotted the ball coolly past Cyprus' goalkeeper and Wales were cruising, leading 2–0 after 23 minutes. But then Cyprus pulled one back ten minutes before half-time after Hennessey misjudged a Cyprus free kick taken from a wide position that curled in towards goal. Attempting to come out and punch it, he missed it marginally and Cyprus were back in it at 2–1. Some fans said Hennessey could have done better, but against Bosnia in the previous game Wales would have been dead and buried without him. How quickly that was seemingly forgotten.

There was another twist in the plot for Wales in the second half, as midfielder Andy King was sent off for a dangerous tackle, so soon after the action restarted that the referee's whistle was still ringing in everyone's ears. Pessimism overwhelmed many supporters at that point – hanging on for 40+ minutes with ten men and a one-goal lead. We'd all been there in similar situations before, when Wales had succumbed to an equaliser or a defeat and everyone was fearing the same outcome here. Despite Cyprus' best efforts, it didn't materialise as ten-man Wales looked pretty comfortable throughout the second half, with the result securing Wales' best start to a group since the Euro 2004 qualifying campaign.

The elation on the faces of the players after the game spoke volumes. Gareth Bale in particular screamed with what looked like a mixture of happiness and relief when the full-time whistle blew. One might think that not scoring in either of the two games would represent a poor performance from Bale, but many people I have spoken to mentioned how inspiring they thought his performances and emotion over the two games were. 'The players' reactions after the game, particularly Gareth Bale's, were hair-raising,' says Dylan Ebenezer, a prominent figure in the Welsh-language media. 'Everybody's jaw dropped when you saw his reaction after the game – you could see how motivated he was. It got everyone thinking, "Well if he's up for it, then the players must be up for it, so we have to be up for it." But the support and the belief over the two games was incredible.'

James Chester, proving to be a great acquisition for Chris Coleman at the heart of the defence, said after the game how comfortable the team felt in holding on to their lead. 'After getting a decent result against Bosnia, we knew it was important that we backed that up with a good result against Cyprus,' said Chester. 'Thankfully, we've got a lot of experience in the squad. I've played in games where we've had to hold on to a lead like that in those circumstances, and I always thought we looked really comfortable and able to do that on the night.'

One of the most endearing things about Chris Coleman is how passionate he is about the Wales team; you just know that even if he wasn't the manager he would be somewhere screaming support for the guys on the pitch. His press conference after the game demonstrated how his emotions reflected those of the fans in the stadium: 'I can safely say looking back now, knowing the result, that I loved it, yeah. I can't say I enjoyed it when I saw that red card come out. My heart sank to be honest. Credit to the lads – we probably wouldn't have won that game in the last campaign. We probably didn't have the same togetherness then as we do now. One defeat in eight – we've got to keep that going.'

Kit Symons praised the Together Stronger campaign for

triggering a change in mentality for the squad. 'These games definitely show how far we've come, but there was a shift of mind-set almost within the camp as well,' said Symons. 'We've got a lot of branding that Ian Gwyn Hughes [head of public affairs], Peter Barnes [media executive] and the FAW have come up with. The Together Stronger campaign is definitely something the players have bought into massively. It's everywhere you turn in camp, real strong images of us as a group. I think we saw the benefits of that campaign in these two games definitely because, even with Andy King sent off, we still thought we'd go on and win it, and to be able to do that was a big achievement for us.'

Jonny Williams, who starred in the first of these two games but sat on the bench in the second, was buoyant about the effect the supporters had on proceedings. 'You can't beat playing in front of a full crowd for your country, it's a really special occasion,' said Williams. 'It's the big stage, the stage we all want to be playing on and to have the whole nation behind you is very important. The atmosphere in both of them games was fantastic, and you can see how much it helped the boys on the pitch, we really want that to continue.'

After this would come Wales' biggest test since their remarkable turn of form began – a clash with a full-strength, motivated Belgium side with as much to play for as Wales. Israel and Wales' impressive starts to the group would surely have got Belgium's attention, so they'd definitely sense the opportunity in the upcoming clash to put an end to Wales' excellent start to the group. For now though, Chris Coleman's men topped the table with seven points. It was a superb position to be in, but Belgium would be the biggest obstacle to that great run continuing into the new year.

Standings after Matchday 2 & 3

Pos.	Team	GP	W	D	L	F	A	GD	Pts
1	Wales	3	2	1	0	4	2	2	7
2	Israel	2	2	0	0	6	2	4	6
3	Belgium	2	1	1	0	7	1	6	4
4	Cyprus	3	1	0	2	4	5	- 1	3
5	Bosnia	3	0	2	1	2	3	- 1	2
6	Andorra	3	0	0	3	2	12	- 10	0

Matchday 2 results:

Wales 0–0 Bosnia & Herzegovina

Cyprus 1–2 Israel

Belgium 6–0 Andorra

Matchday 3 results:

Wales 2–1 Cyprus

Andorra 1–4 Israel

Bosnia & Herzegovina 1–1 Belgium

CHAPTER 10

Belgium vs Wales – 16 November 2014

'They were really well organised. The manager had done his homework. Top work. Belgium was really disappointed, as everyone thought they would beat this team easily.'

KRISTOF TERREUR, BELGIAN FOOTBALL JOURNALIST

WHEN BELGIUM CAME out of the pot at the Euro 2016 qualifying draw and were drawn along with Wales in Group B, a lot of fans were quite satisfied, because Belgium were a team that Wales had played and performed well against fairly recently. As noted earlier, a number of people had picked out the 1–1 draw away at Belgium in late 2013 as the real turning point for Wales under Chris Coleman. They didn't know it at the time of the draw in February, because between the Belgium 2013 game and then, Wales had only played one more game (against Finland) and hadn't had a chance to develop the staggering run they eventually went on, but after an undefeated, yet character-building start to the group, this qualifier in November 2014 would act as a real test of how far Wales had come over the last year or so. A game in the same stadium, against a full-strength Belgium side (as opposed to the slightly weakened XI they'd faced in 2013) would be the perfect test. The team knew it, the fans knew it and the buzz about the game throughout the country illustrated it perfectly.

It's thought that around 6,000 Wales fans made the trip out to Brussels for the game. Wales had only been given 2,500 tickets but people were desperate to be involved. One group of supporters told me they were offered €1,000 for their set of five tickets. People really believed that Wales were going to do well. Belgium hadn't hit top form in the campaign yet and hadn't looked anywhere near their best in the World Cup, despite reaching the quarter-finals. Given the start Wales had managed in the group, many Welsh fans were confident and the number of supporters who made the trip out to Belgium definitely demonstrated that. Once again the FAW's strategy of changing the psychology towards Welsh football to make more fans believe in the side was visible. 'The main aim of this campaign was to get the good start that was required,' said Osian Roberts, 'so that we had points on the board, lifted the doom and gloom, and helped everybody to believe.'

It wasn't all smiles for Wales, though, as this game was played around the time that Gareth Bale was starting to receive what would become a season's worth of dubious criticism and unfair abuse from Real Madrid supporters and those in the media regarding his performances, initially defensively in particular, at club level. Spanish football journalist Graham Hunter felt Bale was suffering from second season syndrome, but confessed he was a fan of Bale's. 'In Gareth's first season I liked everything,' said Hunter. 'His maturity, his attitude to coping with living and working abroad, how he treated joining a massive club like Madrid, how he treated training, how he addressed getting the respect of Ronaldo (which was vital). Then there was his ability to adapt to what was asked of him, 4-3-3 with the ball, 4-4-2 without the ball, and above all, his big game mentality. He was world class in his match psychology – I think he felt unstoppable and it showed in his creativity, work rate, tackling, tactics, it was a joy to watch.'

The criticism of Bale in Spain would become ridiculous later on in the campaign, as Real Madrid's season capitulated. These players know that criticism is part of the job and for someone like Bale I imagine it's just like water off a duck's back, but the criticism of Bale was rarely rounded; he was a scapegoat in my opinion. One of the biggest thrills for Welsh supporters throughout this campaign was how Bale perfectly answered his critics in every game. In this game against Belgium, in the following game against Israel – every time someone had something bad to say about him he made them think twice with some stellar performances – a true world-class player.

What Wales faced in Brussels was a very special team, no doubt about that. It was special in this game; it would be in the reverse fixture in Cardiff the following June, and thanks to the production line they've got going in the country now, it will probably be a very special team for years to come. What speaks most towards how special they are is that they reached the quarter-finals of the World Cup, being knocked out by the eventual runners up, and that was seen as disappointing by some of their own national press and football fans. Most teams would kill for that, especially as a European team in a southern hemisphere World Cup – circumstances that the Europeans have historically not flourished in. That was the scale of the problem that Wales faced in Brussels, a team, a nation so expectant that performing like that in a World Cup wasn't universally seen as good enough.

On paper the average football fan would have said Wales didn't have much of a chance of getting out of Brussels with a win, and only a marginally better one of getting any points at all, but a football game is rarely won or lost by what pieces of paper say, and confidence is a powerful motivator – something Wales had on their side. As Osian Roberts noted, Wales had a lot of experience against Belgium. 'We've always done well against Belgium because they're a typical European side,' said Roberts. 'Although they have a number of very good players, they play a style of football our players are used to. Whereas when we play the likes of Macedonia, Serbia or Croatia, it's different – they're more Latin perhaps, more provocative, very streetwise on the pitch, good game management – frustrating to play against and technically very, very good.'

A big bonus for Wales was that Belgium captain Vincent Kompany missed the game through injury. The Manchester City colossus was widely regarded as one of the best centre-backs in the game so this was welcome news for sure. Also,

Belgium usually played one of two ways – 4–2–3–1 or 4–3–3. Because they're exceptionally good in those systems they don't need to adapt too much. As Roberts said, 'We got it right with Belgium by preparing for the 4-2-3-1. We weren't sure whether they were going with two holding or one but we had prepared for both.' Belgium's line-up wasn't particularly surprising either – Nacer Chadli made the cut, as did Divock Origi who played as a lone striker for Belgium with the likes of Christian Benteke and Romelu Lukaku on the bench. This surprised some, but Origi had performed fairly well for the Red Devils in the World Cup a few months earlier, and was Belgium's joint top-scorer with one goal.

It was a quality group of individuals, then, but not one without problems; problems that the thousands of Welsh fans who had made the trip out were hoping their men could exploit. John Chapman, a Belgian football journalist who has written for the British national papers, detailed the trepidation he was feeling before the game: 'I thought Wales would cause Belgium problems as British teams do,' said Chapman. 'In Bale and Ramsey they had two special talents.'

Wales' two special talents, as Chapman labelled them, did indeed start the game in what was probably their strongest available line-up, and the stage was set – a more or less full-strength Wales against the Belgians, both putting their undefeated streaks in the group on the line. The game kicked off somewhat scrappily with Belgium having the majority of possession, and not necessarily doing anything with it. Given how impressive both teams could be when in possession, spectators didn't see anything like either side's best in the opening phases of the game. Gareth Bale forced the first save after 15 minutes, thanks to a trademark free kick from outside of the box that Thibaut Courtois had to stretch to keep from rifling into the top corner. That's the thing some seemed to overlook with regard to this Belgium team – even if you broke Belgium's outfield players down to the point where you could manage to get a shot off against them, you still had to beat a goalkeeper who, despite being only 22 at the time, had already won the Europa League, League and Cup titles in Spain and Belgium, as well as a host of individual awards for the most clean sheets in a season.

Wales' support was undeterred, though, and kept singing their songs. It was appropriate that the away end was fenced off, somewhat cage-like, from the remaining 48,000 or so fans in the stadium, because Wales' supporters were bouncing around and singing like animals in their section. It really was something amazing to be a part of.

But the biggest test for that support was yet to come, as Bale's effort seemed to spark Belgium's Eden Hazard into life. For the remainder of the half Belgium had numerous shots on target, frequently testing goalkeeper Wayne Hennessey. Hazard had a handful of shots on target and a couple blocked, as did Origi, Chadli and Kevin De Bruyne – some great attacking talent. But it was a defender who went closest to breaking the deadlock for Belgium. Nicolas Lombaerts capitalised on a loose ball in the Wales box following a corner, releasing a fizzing shot towards goal. It was quite a spectacular effort for a defender, especially considering his momentum was taking him away from goal. Thankfully for Wales it struck the post – and the Welsh support held its breath in unison as the ball rebounded into the path of Origi, with Hennessey still recovering position following his attempted save, but the young striker could only knock it out for a goal-kick.

Belgium's movement often causes opposition teams real headaches, and they did their best to punish Wales in this game too. Watching a team move so well and players switch positions so seamlessly is beautiful for a football fan, but when they're doing it against your team you can't help but hate to see it. Origi was everywhere, switching positions with Marouane Fellaini and going up to lead the line sometimes. Hazard was doing his best to blitz everyone on his own. It was quite awesome to see, but in the first half Belgium failed to register on the scoreboard.

On the other hand, nothing gives you more pride as a supporter than to see your team embrace the underdog tag and outwork the favourites, which is what Wales did throughout the campaign, but particularly against Belgium. Chris Coleman has had a fair bit of undue criticism during his Wales tenure, but his ability to come up with tactical solutions to the problems that top teams pose Wales means he deserves to be lavished with praise. In this game Wales were very compact and kept their shape extremely well against a team that was really good at pulling opposition players out of position and, in reality, if it hadn't been for a few marginally misplaced passes or a couple of world-class saves from Courtois, then Wales could have grabbed a goal or two out in Brussels.

This game also, particularly at half-time, saw the birth of what would become one of the highlights of the campaign for Wales fans. When the stadium's PA system started blaring out Zombie Nation's 'Kernkraft 400' – check it out if you haven't heard it – the 2,500 Wales fans in the King Baudouin Stadium went absolutely berserk. Speaking as one of the supporters in the away end that day, I think the reason it sparked such a reaction is because not many of us were expecting anything like that to come on at half-time. British half-time music is usually something generic from the charts, if you're lucky. Hearing this classic dance track, when we were all on cloud nine following the excellent performance on the pitch, just lifted the entire away support even further.

There was more excitement to come as Wales stepped it up another gear in the second half, maintaining their defensive and tactical discipline, but also getting out in numbers in transition more frequently. George Williams came on at the start of the second half, making a real nuisance of himself, and giving Belgium some real problems defensively. Hal Robson-Kanu and Gareth Bale also found more space too, causing Courtois more problems. Belgium's influence waned in the second period because, as good as Hazard was, his domination of possession in the final third for Belgium was causing them problems. Hazard was squeezing De Bruyne out of space. De Bruyne was supposed to be dictating play in a number 10 role, but he was effectively being taken out of the game by his own teammate.

Benteke came on to try and make the difference for Belgium but even he, a beast of a man, couldn't break down Wales' rearguard. He almost did, once, in the very last seconds of the game. Who was there to stop his header going in? Gareth Bale, providing the perfect antidote to the critics who had said he didn't do enough defensive work. He did it when it counted in this game, that's for sure. Following this game, Osian Roberts argued how he couldn't understand the criticism of Bale's defensive work. 'He's the catalyst for us,' said Roberts. 'He's the first player that presses and chases and he's our trigger. If he goes, everyone else goes too. He's great and has a fantastic work-rate. We get all of the players' physical data, the amount of sprints, high-intensity runs, and he's always the highest, without fail. He's developed so much as a person and as a player in this campaign in particular.'

This game certainly was all about the excellent defensive performances on show. The margins were small, and Wales could have won it once or twice, but then the same could be said for Belgium. The draw was the fair result. The most impressive thing about it for Wales was that after four games, Wales had only conceded two goals, and none from open play. Wayne Hennessey, apart from a lapse in concentration against Cyprus, had a brilliant campaign in goal up to this point, but refused to take any credit. 'I'm delighted with our defensive record, hopefully it continues,' said Hennessey. 'I'm always one for giving the defence credit, though. The style of play we have with Wales now is one that really brings the defence into our game since we play everything out from the back. They've had to face some solid strikers so far too: Džeko, Ibišević, Origi, Lukaku, Hazard, Pjanić, etc., so they've done really well.'

James Chester was keen to push praise his 'keeper's way: 'Wayne's been really good when he's been called upon. He's kept us in games, certainly against Bosnia and Belgium. He's made saves where you perhaps wouldn't expect him to and he deserves more plaudits than he gets, especially with the injuries he's had to deal with and still to come back to the top level and performing in the way he has.' Hennessey rarely played for his club side throughout this campaign, which made his stunning Wales form all the more impressive, especially when you consider that he kept Owain Fôn Williams and Danny Ward, two great goalkeepers in their own right, out of the side for the whole campaign.

The praise lavished on Wales didn't merely come from their own, though. Kristof Terreur, who writes for leading Belgian newspaper *HLN*, was impressed with Wales' performance. 'Wales really play as a unit,' he said. 'Tactically they look really strong. I'm always concerned about Gareth Bale. I saw him several times when he played in England and he and Luis Suárez are the players who have impressed me the most since 2013. He just needs one chance.'

Some of Belgium's players weren't as flattering, though, and references were made to Wales 'parking the bus' across their goal. Jan Vertonghen in particular felt Wales had played for the draw. Joe Ledley, in stark contrast, was full of pride for Wales' performance: 'I don't think many people would have thought that the way we set out would have got us the point out there to be honest, which I think was a credit to us that we were actually able to go out and do it and defend this undefeated streak that we have. A massive bonus. It was remarkable, so many fans as well; all of our allocation was sold out, so it was a proud moment for us to go there and get the draw against a world-class team full of top-level Premier League players.'

Substitute goalkeeper Owain Fôn Williams mentioned how tense an experience the game had proved to be from the bench: 'My heart was in my mouth a few times,' he said. 'I was like a kid again. It was great though because I felt like I kicked every single ball that night – absolutely nerve-racking.'

All in all, the game in Brussels capped off a very strong run of performances in the opening round of games. Wales' four opening games had all fallen within a period of just nine weeks and it would be the end of March before the Wales camp got together again. But Chris Coleman spoke of how the nature of the results would only help Wales in the long run: 'In every game so far we've had a bit of adversity and we've handled it really well, no matter what the conditions have been. In each game we've had a bump in the road and we've got over that really well and that speaks to the character of these players. It is fine having the ability in football, but you have to have the mentality as well and the last few months have proved that these players have both.'

While praising the likes of Gareth Bale and Aaron Ramsey, Coleman was quick to throw praise in the direction of the side's other key players. 'The secret to success here is getting players who don't regularly play together, some who don't even regularly play at all, outside of the national side to play like a strong cohesive unit for 90 minutes,' said Coleman. 'Wayne Hennessey has been absolutely wonderful – Chris Gunter, Robson-Kanu, Joe Ledley, Joe Allen, George Williams, Dave Cotterill and so on – it is definitely a collective effort.'

After the game UEFA's Welsh football correspondent Mark Pitman articulated what the result signified for Wales. 'The last 12 months have been about belief,' said Pitman, 'and the side is now back to the level that brought so much optimism under Gary Speed in his final six games in charge. International football is hard, Wales will always need their best players available, but the last 12 months have shown what can be achieved. Many people would have questioned throughout 2012 and 2013 if Wales could ever return to the level that Speed set; however, the last 12 months will only be remembered if the next 12 months follow the same pattern and upward trajectory. There is a new pressure for Chris Coleman and Wales to contend with now, the pressure of expectancy.'

In the city after the game, Wales fans were very keen to

share how they felt about the result. One supporter told me: 'If we hadn't have turned up fully focused today, we'd have been spanked. There's no doubt about it. They threw absolutely everything at us, changed systems a number of times throughout the game and just had options everywhere. But we were so well organised, so, so well organised. The most I've ever celebrated a 0–0 by far!'

The level of Welsh support at the game was recognised by all of the players afterwards, as many of them threw their shirts into the crowd. 'That will probably be a night that I'll look back on when I'm done playing,' said James Chester. 'It was a special night to have so many travelling fans there. To go out there and put on such a good performance for the fans was important.'

Arguably the biggest test of the group, on paper, was now out of the way and Wales had come away with a thoroughly deserved point. Coleman's men were hitting their targets. Wales had planned to be on eight points after four games, and with this result they had managed to secure that so, going into the long wait for the next fixture, they had a lot to be happy about.

Elsewhere in the group, Israel had continued their impressive start by thumping a striker-less and ill-disciplined Bosnia side 3–0 in Haifa, whereas Cyprus had annihilated Andorra 5–0 in Nicosia. In the wake of this round of results, long-mooted rumours of dressing room unrest were all but confirmed as Bosnia & Herzegovina sacked their manager, Safet Sušić, after an uncharacteristically poor start to their qualifying campaign by the remnants of a team that had given Argentina a good run for their money back in June and July's World Cup tournament.

Next up for Wales would be a trip to Haifa to face group-leaders Israel, while Bosnia would face Andorra, and Belgium would host Cyprus. Wales' next game against Israel would be particularly crucial, because three days after that match, Belgium would play their rescheduled fixture in Haifa against the group leaders, meaning that a defeat for Wales there, with other results going a certain way, could see their prospects in the group changing very quickly.

Standings after Matchday 4

Pos.	Team	GP	W	D	L	F	A	GD	Pts
1	Israel	3	3	0	0	9	2	7	9
2	Wales	4	2	2	0	4	2	2	8
3	Cyprus	4	2	0	2	9	5	4	6
4	Belgium	3	1	2	0	7	1	6	5
5	Bosnia	4	0	2	2	2	6	- 4	2
6	Andorra	4	0	0	4	2	17	- 15	0

Results:

Belgium 0–0 Wales

Cyprus 5–0 Andorra

Israel 3–0 Bosnia & Herzegovina

Chapter 11

Israel vs Wales – 28 March 2015

'This game will be the biggest in Welsh football for years, since Russia. Top against second. The next two games are going to dictate whether we finish in the top two or not.'

Chris Coleman, Wales manager

After confirming that Wales' turn in fortunes was no fluke with that excellent draw out in Brussels, Chris Coleman was chomping at the bit to get going again. I met the man himself for the first time a few days after the Belgium game at a local football club where he was opening a new clubhouse and, being a journalism student who loves my football, I just had to get a few minutes to speak with him. What he had to say was somewhat surprising: every question put to him came back to Israel, preparation for the next game, etc. Some might call it short-sighted to be looking at the next game and the next game only, especially when it's such a long time away, but it's totally logical and a big factor in why Wales are always so well prepared and had been doing so well up to this point.

'Don't get me wrong,' began Coleman, 'we'd have preferred to have been playing Israel this week, but the fixtures are the way they are and we have to wait until the end of March. If I had my way we'd have gone to Israel five days after the Belgium game to keep the momentum going. We're taking everything on a game-by-game basis. My target now is to win against Israel then it'll be to win the next one and the next one to put ourselves in the best position to get to France in 2016.'

You could understand the manager wanting to give Israel a lot of attention as, arguably along with Wales, they had been the surprise of the group up to this point, as the third seeds topped the group with three wins from three games. It was obviously built up as first versus second, but more importantly it was third seed versus fourth seed. With most assuming that Belgium would win their game in hand and go on to make first place in the group their own throughout the remaining games, and Bosnia lagging behind after a horrendous start to the group, there was a lot of pressure on both teams to win this one and keep chase with Marc Wilmots' men. Wayne Hennessey was upbeat about the prospect of the game in Haifa. 'We've been surprised with Israel,' he said, 'but the next game now is a fantastic chance for us, especially away. We need to get something out there. What we have to do now is win our home games and take as many points as we can from the away games. We fancy ourselves against any opposition, even the Belgians. We feel strong and confidence is high – teams should be coming to us and thinking "We don't want to be playing Wales right now."'

Members of the media were sceptical of the confidence some were displaying regarding Wales' chances in Haifa and were keen to stress the challenge that Israel presented. 'When the draw came out, everyone was a bit too confident,' outlined Gary Pritchard, part of *Sgorio*'s production team. 'I think there's a danger of us going to Israel and being too confident – the fact that they're top should prevent that though. Because they don't have any huge names in their side, people think that this is going to be an easy six points, but they couldn't be more wrong. The two games against Israel are the two most important in the group. If we're being realistic then Belgium are going to win the group and, provided they get their act together, Bosnia should finish second so we need to beat Israel to secure the play-off spot at the very least.'

A lot of the scepticism seemed to derive from Chris Coleman's comments about it being Wales' biggest game since Russia in 2003. The situation back then had been very similar to Wales' current form up to this point, with Wales unbeaten after four games, flying high, expectations rising. But then it had all gone wrong, and it was in the back of some peoples' minds that it could go wrong again. Nonetheless, if we're talking about omens of 2003, then surely we should point out the fact that the last time Wales qualified for a tournament – 1958 – it was Israel that Wales overcame to get there.

Osian Roberts portrayed a very calm figure, saying Wales were in charge of their own fate. 'Well Bosnia have a new manager so we'll be expecting them to kick on,' he said, 'and they're more than capable of winning their last six games so that would take them to 20 points. They should never be written off. Belgium are equally capable, and Israel are doing very well, so it is going to be very difficult. We're more than capable of beating any of these teams on our day – if we don't get it right tactically though, we are more than capable of losing to all of those teams, so it is in our hands really.'

Some noises coming out of Israel were very boisterous, with one member of their media telling me that they expected to do very well in their games against Wales and Belgium: 'We play very attacking football,' said Raphael Gellar who covers Israeli football for the BBC World Service. 'Our midfield is strong, with the likes of Bibras Natkho, Eran Zahavi, Lior Refaelov and Tal Ben Haim. Damari is the star of the team, our top scorer with five goals in qualifying so far. I'm not surprised we are doing well, but at the same time the only tough team we played is Bosnia, but they had several injured players and you could tell they didn't support their manager. I expect us to beat Wales and hopefully get a point from Belgium.' Expecting to beat the second-placed team in the group and hopeful of a point against one of the best teams in the world, some circles in Israel were clearly very confident.

Personnel-wise, Wales were looking good going into the game. Not one player withdrew from the squad Chris Coleman announced, and Sam Vokes returned after many months out with a cruciate ligament rupture. Vokes noted, like Neil Taylor previously, how Chris Coleman's presence was key to ensuring his recovery went as well as possible. 'When I was injured it showed how good Coleman was as a manager,' said Vokes, 'because he was in touch every couple of months or so on the phone, inviting me down to the camps to do some rehab with the lads, just so I wasn't away from it all really. And then when I came back to full fitness I still felt like I was part of it. It was a nice touch, because when you're stuck in the gym day-in, day-out and you see the squad going out and playing games it was just nice to be down there and be involved.' Vokes' return was a big boost for Wales because he offered the team something that their other forwards perhaps didn't, a real knack for getting on the end of crosses and a really strong aerial presence.

James Chester was the most notable absentee from the provisional squad as he'd failed to recover from a shoulder injury. At the other end of the spectrum for the Wales defence, it was a milestone game for captain Ashley Williams as he won his 50th cap. It was a remarkable achievement considering that since his debut against Luxembourg in 2008, there had only been 57 international fixtures for Wales including this one. Reaching 50 caps in that time would have been unheard of a few years ago when injuries and dropouts were commonplace. Williams had come such a long way from the days when he was the self-confessed 'worst waiter ever', a part-time job he'd undertaken when starting out in the game. Coleman paid tribute to his defender, saying his reaching the 50-cap mark had been inevitable: 'He's a great captain and great leader and what better game to get his 50th in? Ashley's been in the real world. He didn't start at a top Premier League academy or anything – he saw what life is really like. He respects and cherishes every game he plays – that's why he doesn't miss games – he loves his job.'

Criticism of Gareth Bale had reached fever pitch in the build up to this game, as Real Madrid's season was stalling. There had been whispers of criticism throughout the season, but it had gone under the radar somewhat because Carlo Ancelotti's team was in the midst of an incredible 22-game win-streak. Since then, that streak had been snapped, Madrid were struggling by their standards and had very recently suffered losses to fierce rivals Barcelona and Atlético Madrid. Bale, very unfairly, bore the brunt of the criticism that was levelled at the Madrid side, and was the subject of mind games from Israel manager Eli Guttman before the game, who said he thought Bale was saving himself for Wales.

Coleman played down the criticism of the world's most expensive player: 'If he is saving himself for us then it is great for me,' he said. 'When you play for Real Madrid, winning is not enough – you have to entertain too. Gareth's a big boy and he'll come through this, no problem. They'll be thinking about him – I would be. Most teams would be looking at him – whether he's on form or not, he can turn a game on its head. Gareth comes here, he wants to be involved, he's incredibly motivated and he is the last person I am worried about, honestly. I've never been one for mind games. I'd rather get down to business when the whistle blows and see what we can do.'

In the media conferences before the game, some wanted to make a side issue out of the Bale criticism. Neil Taylor, Joe Allen and the returning Sam Vokes were all questioned about Bale's mind-set as much as they were asked about the occasion of the game itself. But, like Coleman, they were very focused while denying there was an issue.

Coleman's handling of his squad was always going to be praised after the way this campaign panned out, but the way he managed the media in this game and in others was brilliant, answering everything with a no-nonsense attitude, but being totally respectful while protecting his side's interests. The way he handled the criticism of Bale is just one such example. He also deftly dealt with the team's injuries and questions regarding the playing style. Balancing expectations, he was remarkable.

Ashley Williams was typically focused in spite of his impending milestone as he talked of the advantage he believed Wales' preparation gave them. 'I'm obviously aware that it's my 50th,' he said. 'It's something I'll enjoy after the game, probably.

I'm just focusing on getting the job done in the 90 minutes, really. We start with a point so if we leave with a point that's good, too, but that's not our mentality. We want to win the game. We understand there are going to be periods in the game when we have to do a lot of defending because they are a good team, but we feel that the way that we prepare means we have enough in there to get the win.'

A thousand Wales fans made the hefty trip to Haifa for the game, obviously sensing the occasion in front of them, and any talk of the Israelis being intimidating was thrown out of the window straight away by the efforts of the Welsh faithful, who were as vociferous as any away crowd in world football. You could understand some trepidation creeping in, given the political situation in the country and the occasion, but the Wales fans didn't show any concerns about that. There was a huge 'Chris Coleman's Barmy Army' flag adorning the Wales end – a dramatic turnaround from the booing of him at half-time in Andorra – as well as a sea of Wales flags emblazoned with town names such as Bagillt, Llandudno, Swansea and Pwllheli, representing the entirety of Wales.

As passionate and knowledgeable as the supporters are, not many among them would have predicted the team that Coleman and his backroom staff selected. Joe Ledley spoke of the obvious benefits of being tactically adaptable. 'It's very good when you mix the formation up,' said Ledley, 'especially in terms of the opposition because they don't know what we're going to play so they have a much tougher time against us. We have mixed it up going 4–2–3–1, 4–4–1–1, three at the back so, yeah, we have changed but it is good. It is great for us because we've adapted really well to it. It's beneficial from another perspective too, because when we turn up we don't even know ourselves what system we're going to play until we do the build-up a few days before kick-off. So it's good because it keeps us on our toes. I certainly don't think Israel were expecting us to go with the set-up that we did.'

Everyone was kept on their toes with this one, as Wales had

gone back to their wing-back system with a 3–4–2–1; few had envisaged three centre-backs being used with James Chester out injured, so it's fair to say some were taken aback by the selection. Wayne Hennessey started in goal again. Ashley Williams earned his 50th cap at centre-back alongside James Collins, who was making his first start of the campaign, and Ben Davies with the trio flanked by Chris Gunter and Neil Taylor in the wing-back positions. Joe Allen and Joe Ledley filled the deeper positions in midfield, whereas Aaron Ramsey and Bale sat behind Hal Robson-Kanu up front to complete the XI.

The interchanging and movement of the whole team, as the system changed moderately throughout the match, but particularly the front three and their link-up play, would be crucial to Wales' success in this game. Sometimes Bale went to join Robson-Kanu up front, sometimes Ramsey. Sometimes Ramsey dropped into midfield, but the way they worked together was crucial, as the 90 minutes that followed would go a long way to proving that the Red Dragons had what it took to reach Euro 2016.

Playing such an unusual system was a no-brainer for Wales, according to assistant manager Kit Symons. 'It wasn't necessarily the three centre-backs that made us want to do it; we pick a formation where we can get our best players doing the most damage,' said Symons. 'So a big part of the 3–4–2–1 was the box in midfield with the two Joes holding and Ramsey and Bale in front as two number 10s. You'd be hard pushed to find two number 10s as good as those two, which was one of the main reasons we wanted to go with that system in that game. That formation with the personnel worked perfectly. We had the centre-backs who were comfortable with it, the wing-backs who were mobile enough to do it, so it just suited us perfectly.'

As a spectacle, this game was always going to be pretty special. Wales' support didn't do anything by halves in this campaign, whereas the Israeli faithful were a passionate bunch too, especially so considering their position in the group. To see the two sets of supporters throwing their all behind their teams from the second they stepped out onto the pitch was incredible. To call it a cauldron of noise inside Haifa's Sammy Ofer Stadium is a bit of a cliché, but it's certainly very apt in this case as the rapturous atmosphere, befitting of the occasion, was spine-tingling. This fuelled Wales, who started the better of the two teams with the wing-backs getting forward very early on. The work Taylor, Gunter and others did in the wing-back positions in this campaign was so overlooked by the majority of people, despite the fact that they probably covered more ground than anyone and were absolutely rampant in helping Wales on both ends of the pitch. They certainly gave the Israelis something to think about out wide, because the defensive plan from the outset for Israel seemed to be to keep Gareth Bale, Aaron Ramsey and Joe Allen within arm's length at all times. The fact that those three players all had a case for Man of the Match at full time perhaps tells you just how poorly Israel's defensive strategy fared.

Everything was very slick, both teams wanted to pass it around, both teams wanted to press the ball. Wales were having more of the ball in Israel's final third than Israel were in Wales', and Coleman's men were ahead in terms of shots on goal, but still it was a fairly even contest in the opening exchanges. James Collins had the first real chance of the match. Having stayed in Israel's final third following a corner, he wandered back into the box to meet a Gareth Bale cross, found himself seemingly through on an open goal and only had to get some kind of contact on the ball to knock it in. Incredibly though, Collins managed to slide his foot over the ball rather than hit it, so the ball ended up behind him and the chance had gone.

If there was any tension still in the air about Wales' ability to perform when the pressure was on, that miss surely exacerbated it. In truth, though, Wales had the game well under control in the first half. Joe Allen's new moniker, the Welsh Xavi, was looking prudent in this game, as he pulled the strings throughout the first half with movement between Bale, Ramsey, Robson-Kanu and the energy of the Welsh wing-backs leaving the Israeli defence in a bit of a whirlwind at times. Taylor and Gunter were key to Wales' pressing efforts, too, in this game, as they had been throughout the campaign. They were often seen as high as the halfway line whenever Wales lost possession in the opposition half, ready to press and win it back, or shuffle the opposition into the middle of the pitch where the central midfielders could sweep things up.

The home side created a couple of good chances of their own in the remainder of the half, but Wales soon got their rewards for such a confident performance in ironic circumstances. Having played such a fluent short-passing game throughout the first half, Hennessey opted for a change of tactics as half-time approached by belting the ball from the edge of his box into the Israeli final third. With Gareth Bale, Hal Robson-Kanu and Aaron Ramsey all positioning themselves within about ten feet of each other in a triangle on the edge of the box ready to react, Bale, running backwards, got on the end of Hennessey's delivery with a header and was able to put just enough power into it to find the onrushing Aaron Ramsey completely unmarked. Ramsey sent a header of his own looping over the Israeli goalkeeper and into the back of the net for Wales to get the lead with practically the last touch of the first half. Pointing to the sky in memory of his grandmother who had passed away the weekend before, Ramsey ran over to the delirious Welsh faithful to celebrate the lead with them. Route One, direct football, had put Wales in the lead. Who'd have thought it? Whether you believed the challenge of Israel was overstated or not, it was the first time they'd been behind having played 315 minutes of football in the group up to this point. So it was no mean feat by Wales to put Israel on the back foot and in uncharted territory for the second half. Could Israel respond?

If Wales' first-half performance had been confident, their second-half performance was purely ruthless, with the game over as a contest just five minutes after the action recommenced. The atmosphere was still electric, absolutely incredible, but within five minutes of coming out for the second half Wales had totally silenced the crowd; apart, that is, from a small corner of the ground where everyone was dancing around like lunatics. No prizes for guessing which fans were sat there.

Bale was the instigator, winning and converting a free kick that left Israel 'keeper Ofir Marciano rooted to the spot, putting Wales 2–0 up on the night. His efforts in this game were a perfect answer to his critics, and his passionate celebration demonstrated that, as he had practically made certain of a vital victory for his country in their quest to make history.

Eytan Tibi, booked for the foul on Bale that led to Wales' second goal, received a second booking and was sent off soon afterwards, which all but guaranteed Wales victory. Bale got his second and Wales' third later on, in a move that epitomised their performance. Ramsey dribbled into the left-hand side of the Israel box, throwing in a couple of step-overs to disguise an incisive pass across the box towards Bale, who was able to run into space between four Israel players near the penalty spot and lash the ball home. Far too slick, far too powerful, far more desire and – apart from Collins' unbelievable miss – only needing half a chance, Wales had brushed Israel aside with an exceptional performance in Haifa, earning a rampant 3–0 victory.

Some were surprised by the manner of Wales' victory in this game, not least those in the deflated Israeli media. 'Wow, where to begin,' said Raphael Gellar. 'We didn't start the right players, we didn't play smart tactics and we didn't give enough respect to Wales. No-one expected Wales to be so physical. I was very surprised with that. Bottom line, Wales were faster, stronger, more prepared and more talented. Ashley Williams was a rock tonight. He's so underrated, but we gave far too much space to Bale and Ramsey too.'

However Chris Wathan of Wales Online wasn't surprised at all. 'It hasn't surprised me, not one iota,' he said, 'because the ability has been there, the experience of so many players now. The likes of Neil Taylor and Ashley Williams have got four years of Premier League and Europa League experience behind them. Ramsey is playing in the Champions League regularly. Chris Gunter is approaching 60 caps. You've got a manager more comfortable and confident going forward. Bale being Bale, you know you've always got a chance. I think everything combined added up to the fact that it was all set up for them and they've taken their chances so far.'

It was Wales' first show of ruthlessness in the group and a fitting time for it to happen, not only for the significance of the result within the group, but also in order to pay tribute to the passing of one of the most important members of the Wales set-up, kit man Dai Williams, who had passed away the month before the game against Israel, with all of the Wales squad wearing black armbands during the game in his memory.

After building up the game so much beforehand, Wales' manager was naturally very pleased that his team had performed so well, but unsurprisingly was already looking to the next game. 'It's a great result,' said Coleman. 'A wonderful performance. The pleasing thing for me is seeing the team implementing the style of play they've worked on all week. Sometimes you play really well and you don't get the result, so we needed to concentrate on the performance and we did that and it was a great performance. Israel are a good team. It's a difficult place to come, big crowd, very passionate. We needed to keep them quiet, stay in the game, keep calm, keep composed. We stood up to anything they had in the first half and controlled the tempo of the game. We won 3–0 but I don't think anyone could have complained if we'd won by more but our biggest result is yet to happen. I believe it will happen and I believe it will be in this campaign.' Instant focus on the next challenge, yet again.

Coleman wasn't the only one who believed Wales' biggest result – qualifying for a major tournament – would happen, after such an emphatic victory. Making it look easy against the group leaders as you swat them aside 3–0 is going to inspire confidence from your fan-base, and it certainly did from my perspective as this was the game where I, and many other supporters, commentators and players, really started to believe that Wales would qualify for France. It wasn't just a 3–0 win; it was a total annihilation. Wales' dragons were flying high, and they didn't look like coming back down to earth any time soon.

The result put Wales at the top of Group B for a few days, before Belgium travelled to Israel to play their rescheduled fixture from the previous September. Their 1–0 win set up another first versus second clash to come in Cardiff in a few months' time, as Wales would host Belgium and Wales fans would see if Chris Coleman's aforementioned belief was truly well-placed or not.

Standings after Matchday 5

Pos.	Team	GP	W	D	L	F	A	GD	Pts
1	Belgium	5	3	2	0	13	1	12	11
2	Wales	5	3	2	0	7	2	5	11
3	Israel	5	3	0	2	9	6	3	9
4	Cyprus	5	2	0	3	9	10	- 1	6
5	Bosnia	5	1	2	2	5	6	- 1	5
6	Andorra	5	0	0	5	2	20	- 18	0

Results:
Israel 0–3 Wales
Andorra 0–3 Bosnia & Herzegovina
Belgium 5–0 Cyprus
Israel 0–1 Belgium

CHAPTER 12

Wales vs Belgium – 12 June 2015

'Thinking about the journey we've had from losing
6–1 to Serbia to where we are now is incredible,
and Chris Coleman deserves a lot of credit for that.'

ASHLEY WILLIAMS, WALES CAPTAIN

AS FOOTBALL FANS, we've all witnessed our teams take part in elaborate marketing campaigns to try and make everyone feel like they're part of a common cause. Usually these campaigns are pretty hollow and no-one cares about them whatsoever. 'More than a number', 'Believe', 'Part of the family' – they've become almost overused clichés by now. None of them worked anything like as well as Wales' 'Together Stronger' and, for many who were involved, this game was the embodiment of what that marketing campaign was about.

The atmosphere at the Cardiff City Stadium during the match against Belgium was by far the most electrifying that any of the 33,000 fans there had ever experienced. Everyone said so – even the Belgians. Afterwards Twitter was awash with capital letters and exclamation marks regarding the result, the atmosphere, the anthems – quite simply, this game caused a buzz like nothing any Wales fan had experienced for years. The games to follow might have been equally crazy in terms of atmosphere, but this was the first to reach such an unbelievable level, which is probably why so many people lauded the occasion in the weeks and months that followed.

The FAW did their best to ensure this kind of atmosphere, laying on a performance by the Super Furry Animals. A big

'Cymru' tifo in the colours of the Welsh flag was displayed by the Canton End fans before kick-off, and clappers were attached to every seat that opened out to say 'Come on Wales'. The Barry Horns brass band were also there to help sustain an amazing atmosphere into the last 20 minutes of the game. It was an enormous occasion, perhaps the biggest in Welsh football history. If the result went Wales' way, it would certainly be the biggest win for a long time.

Over the course of the campaign, the Welsh support had indeed become stronger together. Following the Andorra away game there had been a sense of 'Phew, we made it'. The Bosnia and Cyprus home games saw fans realise how far Wales had come in terms of game management in adverse circumstances. Brussels confirmed to everyone that Wales had the ability to go to the most difficult places in the world and grind out a result, and at Haifa, where the Welsh faithful saw their first real show of ruthlessness from Wales under Chris Coleman, people really started to believe en masse.

The Euro 2016 qualifying campaign up to this point could be seen as a miniature Chris Coleman version of Wales' earlier six-phase plan. Wales had learned and implemented many lessons throughout each of the five games so far, and a positive result in the sixth would mean they were thoroughly in control of their own destiny. Even a negative result wouldn't have been the end of the world. However some supporters were uneasy, as it was yet to be seen how this squad, having gone on such an exceptional run of form, might deal with defeat having only lost once since October 2013. It was an entirely subjective opinion, most likely borne out of the failures of Wales' teams in the past in these pressure situations, but a somewhat understandable one.

Going into this game, Wales decided against playing a preparatory friendly. Coleman and his team decided that there would be no point playing a team that didn't offer similar challenges to the problems Belgium would pose them in this game. It would be fair to say that Wales' fans weren't disappointed with the resulting two weeks of solid preparations with no distractions. Belgium, however, did play a friendly against a top side in the form of recent World Cup quarter-finalists, France, in Paris. Someone must have forgotten to tell Belgium it was a friendly, though, because they absolutely eviscerated France in that game. A 4–3 victory for Belgium may sound close, but for the first 70 minutes the game most definitely wasn't, as Belgium led 4–1, completely ran the show and only conceded two goals in the dying embers of the game after Belgian substitutions weakened the shape of the team.

The performance resulted in praise being lavished upon the Belgians by some of the Welsh press. BBC Wales Sports' Dafydd Pritchard, who was at the game in the Stade de France, hailed the opening 70 minutes as the best performance he'd ever seen from Belgium, with many in agreement that it was their most impressive performance since before the World Cup. And all without one of their best players, who would return to play Wales, the German Bundesliga's players' Player of the Year, Kevin De Bruyne.

One might have expected Wales to be in awe of a Belgium side that had dismantled such a good team, but that wasn't the case. In a pre-match press conference, Osian Roberts, who had travelled with Chris Coleman to the game in Paris, pointed out that there were weaknesses to exploit in the Belgium team. 'They did concede three so there's a question mark there from our viewpoint,' said Roberts. 'We've played five games and five different systems but every time we play Belgium we play the same way and it has worked. We know their strengths and we'll be aware of those.' Recalling the reverse fixture, Roberts added that had Wales been better in transition in that game then they would have given Belgium a lot more to think about. This was something Wales worked on extensively in their preparations for this game, so that when opportunities arose for counters they could exploit them better.

What would have encouraged Wales further was Belgium's lack of defensive assuredness down the flanks against France, something Wales were more than capable of exploiting with their pace. Vincent Kompany would miss this game as well, having been sent off in Belgium's last game against Israel and Marouane Fellaini picked up an injury in the week building up to the game. Many pointed to these two absentees as big plusses for Wales, but Kompany had also missed the game against France and been replaced by young Jason Denayer who had displayed an impressive level of composure. This was something else picked up on pre-match – was Denayer someone Wales could look to exploit, given his inexperience? Roberts was quick to shoot that down. 'Did you see Denayer play on the weekend?' asked Roberts. 'He was outstanding, absolutely outstanding. Kompany is of course the leader and the experienced one but this boy was outstanding in a game of that magnitude, a more than adequate replacement.'

Roberts had been exceptionally calm in his press conference, as usual, speaking in a very measured manner. Chris Coleman mirrored this approach, but had to deal with a lot more pro-Belgium questions, partly because there were more Belgian journalists in attendance at his conference, but also because it was so close to the game and this is what everyone seemingly wanted to talk about. Towards the end of Coleman's conference he was asked by the Belgian press about Radja Nainggolan, who had played particularly well in Paris but had not played in the first game against Wales back in November. Asked if he was an unknown quantity to Wales as a result, Coleman responded in a defiant way that drew a lot of laughter from everyone in the room. 'Oh no, no,' he said. 'We know about all your players, don't worry about that. He's a good player and he played well in that game. You know as well as I do that you could change four players in that team and not lose anything in terms of performance. We've spoken a lot about Belgium, but they'll need to concentrate on us Friday night because we won't just be inviting you guys into our backyard and letting you get on with it – we'll have something to say for sure.'

The way the game was being built up, with a lot being made of Belgium almost to the point where Wales were being overlooked, was much like it had been before the Brussels game, when the Belgian nation had expected their team to turn Wales over quite easily. But this hadn't happened – and Coleman was adamant that people shouldn't think that it was going to happen this time around, either.

Some may have doubted Coleman's credentials after he took the job, and criticised how long it had taken him to turn such a horrible situation around, but he had every right to have such confidence in his own and his team's abilities. He'd inherited essentially a heartbroken nation and produced a team now placed just outside the top 20 FIFA rankings. That confidence, which shone through particularly in this campaign, endeared him to so many of the doubters he initially had and turned them into vociferous supporters.

Even without three centre-backs in James Collins, Ben Davies and Paul Dummett – as well as other players such as Jonny Williams, Emyr Huws and George Williams – Coleman was still up for the fight. Chris Wathan also picked up on Coleman's defiance. 'He wasn't messing,' said Wathan. 'Now and again in his press conferences, you can almost imagine him rolling his sleeves up with the smile and a snarl of an old warrior centre-back, and there was a sense of that about him that day. He spoke with a smile but there was serious intent there. And I think the players respond to that side of Coleman.'

If Wales' press conferences generally reflected a calm, reassuring approach – in terms of Wales knowing what they faced and knowing what they had to do to overcome it – Belgium's press conference the day before the game was totally different. Thibaut Courtois spoke first, followed by Marc Wilmots. Both addressed the Belgian media first in French. None of the Welsh media could understand a word, but a few of the journalists could be seen tweeting jokes about names or words they recognised, perhaps to lighten the mood because there was a lot of tension in the way Courtois and Wilmots spoke, which raised a few eyebrows. Were they nervous? Maybe. Maybe not. The line of questioning may have just annoyed them. Either way, they didn't seem as comfortable nor as confident as some expected them to be.

As this campaign rolled out the Welsh fans felt more confident and comfortable about the tactical adaptability of Chris Coleman's team, especially after the 3–0 demolition of Israel where the 3–4–2–1 seemed to catch a lot of people off-guard. Picking that system in that game had raised a few eyebrows. Picking it against Belgium this time seemed out of the question given Wales' absentees, but Coleman's team thought differently. The decision was taken to stick with the unusual system, with Jazz Richards making his campaign debut at right-wing-back, and Chris Gunter shifting inside to right-centre-back with Ashley Williams, James Chester and Neil Taylor making up the rest of the back five.

An injury to Paul Dummett in training hadn't forced Wales to change any of their preparations too drastically, according to Kit Symons. 'There was a temptation to go for a flat back-four,' admitted Symons, 'but we sat down and spoke about it and I was keen for Jazz to get in, because I'd had him on loan at Fulham and knew how good he was and that he'd be more than capable of doing that role. Gunter had played as part of a centre-back pairing against Belgium in a previous campaign, so we knew he'd be OK in a three because it's theoretically easier for him. So there were a few changes but we were that confident in the personnel that we didn't think it would matter to shift their roles about a bit.'

The usual suspects made up the rest of the team, with Hal Robson-Kanu leading the line, Gareth Bale, winning his 50th cap on quite an occasion, and Aaron Ramsey behind him. Joe Ledley and Joe Allen – both a booking away from missing the next match against Cyprus – sat behind. The choice of system divided opinion initially, as some were very sceptical. Social media was awash with people questioning the decision but, if anything, the line-up was a great show of intent and could possibly have caught Belgium off guard, since it was a system that could exploit the weaknesses Belgium displayed against France. Coleman said he wasn't going to invite Belgium in to let them have their way and picking this system definitely showed that intent.

The Belgian side that took to the field in Cardiff included four changes from the side that had played in Brussels as Jason Denayer, Radja Nainggolan, Dries Mertens and Christian Benteke featured this time around, in the same 4–2–3–1 system, in place of Anthony Vanden Borre, Marouane Fellaini, Nacer Chadli and Divock Origi. Not bad changes at all.

When the Red Devils arrived at the Cardiff City Stadium, they were in for one big surprise. The FAW had pleaded on social media throughout the week for as many fans as possible to arrive at the stadium by 7pm to cheer the team through the warm-up and build the atmosphere towards the kick-off. Of course, the fans responded and the stadium was pretty full by the time the Super Furry Animals performed 'Fire In My Heart' – such an appropriate song given that the campaign to date had rejuvenated the fire in the nation's hearts for the first time in a long time. The crowd sensed the opportunity for a big result in this game. The atmosphere was unfamiliar. There was a confidence, a real buzz about the place. Unlike many previous Wales games, there wasn't much tension in the air. It was a party atmosphere, perhaps because Zombie Nation, a fan favourite from the reverse fixture, was again played around the ground. All in all it didn't feel anything like the build-up to a game of such magnitude. Everyone was up for the show, and both teams certainly gave them one.

I say there was no tension but perhaps that was only true until the Welsh faithful cranked up the volume as the game kicked off. There was such an awesome racket when the players emerged from the tunnel and the anthem was bellowed out passionately by everyone – quite possibly reflecting the nerves that the fans had managed to suppress so far. The Belgium players, however, were totally undeterred by the deafening noise of the Welsh fans, and dominated the possession in the opening phases of the game with Nainggolan the focal point of their attack, pulling the strings from his central position. He recycled play constantly, with Hazard and Mertens busy down the flanks. De Bruyne, finding more space in the early stages of this game compared to the Brussels fixture, looked very busy as well, but Belgium's execution in the final third was wasteful. Mertens was the first to test the Wales backline, with an early cross in from the right to find Christian Benteke, but the towering striker couldn't connect with it. Benteke's battle with Ashley Williams would be one of the highlights of the evening.

Gareth Bale then made the first inroads into an area in which Wales would find a lot of joy throughout the evening, attacking Jan Vertonghen down the flank. A total mismatch in pace resulted in a corner, but more would come for Wales from those situations later on in the game. Meanwhile Nainggolan was still pulling the strings for Belgium, testing Hennessey with a fizzing shot from outside the box which forced a great save out of the goalkeeper. At this point you could sense the tension growing, as the crowd seemed to hold their breath every time Belgium entered the final third.

With only 15 minutes gone, the memories of Belgium's 2–0 win over Wales in the last campaign were flooding back, but Wales, deflecting, blocking and fighting for every ball, grew into the game. The wing-backs were the key. After the game Ashley Williams would note how essential Swansea duo Jazz Richards and Neil Taylor had been in helping Wales weather that early storm. 'The wing-backs played a big part offensively, but the biggest job they had to do tonight was stopping the crosses coming in,' said Williams. 'I don't know how many they stopped, but there were so many, especially early on.' Quite apart from their defensive effort, Taylor and Richards were also getting forward and caused Belgium many problems down the flanks.

It's one of the most frustrating things in football when your team has quality in almost every area but struggles constantly in just one. This was exactly what was happening to Belgium. Wales were attacking the flanks in numbers and Belgium's full-backs were struggling to cope. The Red Dragons had the Red Devils on the ropes for a period and they weren't going to let their advantage go without doing their best to draw first blood. More good work down the flanks saw the tireless Hal Robson-Kanu win a free kick near the corner flag. Belgium half-cleared Aaron Ramsey's delivery, and the ball ping-ponged around the edge of the box before finding the head of the excellent Nainggolan. In a moment of madness, one the midfielder would probably never repeat if given the opportunity to relive the scenario a thousand times over, Nainggolan attempted to head the ball back from outside his own box over a number of opposition players and teammates to his goalkeeper, but got it horribly wrong. A dragon was there waiting to pounce, the most ferocious dragon of them all. One-on-one with one of the best goalkeepers in the world, Gareth Bale slotted the ball home through Courtois' legs, making it look easy. Chaos ensued.

I wouldn't call it noise, because it was so much more than that. It was stranger-hugging, jumping around, open-mouthed incredulity. Could Wales really start to believe? It wasn't just that Wales had scored, but the fact that Belgium had made a glaring error under pressure. This was something that historically Wales might have done, but were instead now forcing one of the the world's top teams to do. And they were making them pay for it.

Now came the agonising wait. Sixty-five minutes – although it felt more like 65 years – of nail-biting, eye-covering and breath-holding. While the belief in Wales' ability was increasing by the game, the belief that Belgium could quite easily turn this around if Wales allowed them to start firing on all cylinders hadn't exactly diminished in the aftermath of the Bale goal. But the Red Devils didn't have the chance to show it throughout the rest of the half, as the Welsh wing-backs were still menacing away down the flanks. Pinning the Belgians back, they created a couple of great chances for Wales to double their lead which, unfortunately, couldn't be capitalised upon.

Half-time arrived, a well-deserved breather for the men involved on the pitch but also for the 33,000 in the stands who certainly needed to take stock after that half. According to Neil Taylor the first half had gone as close to plan for Wales as it possibly could have done. 'It was hard graft because we didn't see a lot of the ball,' said Taylor. 'But we knew we weren't going to. We always felt that if we got a goal that would be it, because we're a team that is so determined not to concede that we give ourselves a good chance, and it went to plan. They've got players who can win the game like that, but we kept it tight and I don't think we conceded too many clear-cut chances.'

Where Wales had clearly worked hard on improving certain aspects of their game since the reverse fixture, Belgium hadn't raised their level at all. It was too late to change that now, though – what they needed was new ideas. As the second half kicked off Romelu Lukaku entered the game for Mertens, as Belgium switched to 4-4-2, hoping that two behemoths would be more effective than one in connecting with the plethora of crosses that Belgium were attempting to make into the box. But the three Wales centre-backs were like men possessed, as practically nothing got past them, never mind past Wayne Hennessey in the Wales goal.

It got a bit hairy in the second half with Wales having to deal with corner after corner in the opening ten minutes, struggling to get out of their defensive third at times and inviting pressure onto themselves. But once again, the fans provided the perfect lift. Belgium had been on the front foot for most of the second half, and with 70 minutes gone they were on the attack again. Wales had been forced to defend quite deep at times and the fans knew that their dragons couldn't afford Belgium that advantage. Just as their men on the pitch needed that extra push to hold Belgium out, the most passionate rendition of the Welsh national anthem started up among the diehards in the Canton End. As everyone with Welsh blood in their veins joined in, it was soon ringing around the entire stadium. Ben Dudley, a lifelong Wales fan who writes the most evocative match reports, said afterwards, 'It was the most powerful impact I have ever seen a crowd make on a football game. After that moment I knew we had won. Welsh football was back from the dead and our time had come. Not even the team that wins the European Championships next year will have a moment like that.'

Ashley Williams was having the game of his life, doing absolutely nothing wrong, but after that point he caught his second wind, it seemed, and kept making life impossibly difficult for Benteke and Lukaku. Everyone performed exceptionally, though, not just the defenders. Gareth Bale, long acknowledged as one of the fittest, fastest, most athletic players on the planet, ended up going off after 88 minutes with cramp; absolutely unheard of, but a testament to the immense effort the prince of Wales had contributed on this glorious night for Welsh football.

Added time felt like an extra 90 minutes in itself, but it eventually passed and the immense spectacle was over. Wales had exceeded the expectations of many and, after another exceptional tactical display, had walked away with a 1–0 win against the second-best team in the world. Apart from a quiet little corner where the Belgian fans were seated, the entire stadium went mad in celebration of an epic victory. This was a bigger win than Spain in 1985, Germany in 1991 or Italy in 2002. This game put Wales' Euro '16 destiny firmly within their own grasp. The fans knew it and even the pessimists among them were starting to imagine what France would be like. On the pitch, however, there was unity and serenity as the players and coaching staff came together for a post-match huddle. They knew the job wasn't done, only that their dream was a step closer to being realised and that more of the same was needed in the coming months if it were to come true.

After the game Chris Coleman was typically modest in victory. It says a lot about him as a man that he could have quite easily taken a lot more of the credit for the way the side's fortunes had turned around up to this point, yet he refused to do so. For far too long as Wales manager he hadn't been given the respect he'd deserved, and even though now people were trying to give it to him he was still deflecting praise, crediting everyone else for their involvement. 'We're going to enjoy this tonight,' Coleman told the media. 'The players and the staff and the Welsh public should enjoy it and get excited. We're not going to play that down. We're just going to have to live up to expectations. We've been chipping away for a long time and my staff are absolutely fantastic – they work so hard to gain the odd 1 per cent in performance here and there. We work hard for that and I'm delighted for my staff and of course the players.'

The most important thing Coleman had to say, though, was this: 'The rankings are very healthy so what we've got to do now is not play it down. Let's not say "Oh, we've been here before." We know we've been here before but this is our own journey. We're trailblazing in many ways, really, so we've just got to keep marching on.' A lot of people loved hearing Coleman say that. It was a real show of intent and belief from the manager, echoing the belief of the players and the fans that he had helped kick-start so many months ago.

Ashley Williams was full of praise for his manager. 'I don't think the performance is a message to the rest of Europe, I think it is a message to ourselves that if we work hard and perform then we can get results like this,' said Williams. 'I think we've realised we are actually a good team. I think the way we leave it out there on the line for each other is what does it for us. I don't think the manager gets enough credit, really. To turn it around, thinking about the journey we've had from losing 6–1 to Serbia to where we are now, is incredible and Chris Coleman deserves a lot of credit for that.'

While there had been jokes on Twitter before the game about how Eden Hazard would probably never have even heard of Jazz Richards, it was clear that he knew all about him afterwards. Richards, in his campaign debut, had given him an exceptionally tough game down that flank. 'Yeah, I thought I did alright tonight,' said Richards afterwards. 'I stopped the crosses when I had to, and kept the ball when I had to. I found out midweek I would be playing and I was thinking they wouldn't be expecting to see me out there, probably expecting to see Chris [Gunter] out there with someone else at centre-back. I tried my best to keep Hazard quiet, obviously he's world-class, but I think I did what I had to do.' In truth, Richards had been paramount to Wales keeping alive their astounding record of not conceding from open-play in this campaign. Six games had been played now and only two goals conceded, both from set-pieces. Staggering.

Of course, at the other end of the pitch, Gareth Bale had made the crucial difference for Wales; a perfect night for him winning his 50th cap, scoring the winning goal. 'I think we all stepped up for the occasion and did what we had to do,' said Bale after the game. 'It was a very special occasion for me, very emotional too with all of my family and friends here. I say in every interview: we literally have the best fans in the world – I've not experienced many atmospheres like that in my whole career. We're not there yet, but we'll enjoy the result of course. Come the next bunch of games we'll be focused and ready to go – it's easy to get carried away with this, but we still need to be focused.'

The party in the city was as if Wales had qualified. Everyone seemed to forget that there were still four more games to play after this one. Elsewhere in the group, Bosnia had beaten Israel 3–1 and Wales' next opponent, Cyprus, had won 3–1 away at Andorra. But Wales would have to face Cyprus without their 'Welsh Xavi' Joe Allen, as he'd picked up a booking in this game and would be suspended for the next match as a result. Those fixtures wouldn't come for another three months, but it was a certainty that the fans at least would be celebrating this result from the final whistle of this game to the kick-off of the next, and beyond.

To top off what had been an amazing 90 minutes for Welsh football, Wales were about to accomplish another incredible feat. It was all but confirmed after the game that if Wales won, they would be among the top seeds for the upcoming World Cup draw on 25 July – the first team ever to go from Pot 6 in one World Cup draw to Pot 1 in the next. Amazing, absolutely incredible. And, as if that weren't enough, thanks to a favour from their Argentinian/Patagonian cousins in the Copa America final ensuring Chile vs Argentina would go to extra time, Wales would be ranked as one of the top ten teams in international football for the first time ever. Chris Coleman had said the team was trailblazing – he hadn't got much wrong up to this point in the campaign at all, and he definitely wasn't wrong in this regard. It was an absolutely staggering achievement.

Kit Symons, a key factor in Wales' success under Chris Coleman, would leave the set-up after this game to focus full time on his managerial position at Fulham FC. He'd taken the job with Coleman in such horrific circumstances, but was glad he had done so. 'Yeah I'm 100 per cent happy that I did it,' said Symons. 'Playing for your country is the pinnacle, but the next best thing is coaching or managing your country. Not many people can say they've done both. It made it sweeter, I suppose, that my best mate was my manager, and sweeter still that we went through those really tough times and then suddenly we're top ten in the world. To go out on that Belgium game was amazing, and I'm still devastated having to not do it any more, but I couldn't be prouder of the job that was done while I was there.'

Wales would go on without him, as Paul Trollope came in and Osian Roberts was promoted to assistant manager, but Symons' contribution would not be forgotten.

Standings after Matchday 6

Pos.	Team	GP	W	D	L	F	A	GD	Pts
1	Wales	6	4	2	0	8	2	6	14
2	Belgium	6	3	2	1	13	2	11	11
3	Israel	6	3	0	3	10	9	1	9
4	Cyprus	6	3	0	3	12	11	1	9
5	Bosnia	6	2	2	2	8	7	1	8
6	Andorra	6	0	0	6	3	23	- 20	0

Results:

Wales 1–0 Belgium

Bosnia & Herzegovina 3–1 Israel

Andorra 1–3 Cyprus

CHAPTER 13

Gaining a mental edge, the frontier that Wales had to conquer to get to France

'People say the psychological side of the game is so important but how often do they train for that every week? They say it's a huge part but they never work on it.'

IAN MITCHELL, WALES PERFORMANCE PSYCHOLOGIST

WE'VE TALKED A lot about the adversity that the Wales side had endured during this Euro 2016 qualifying campaign, ever since the first minute against Andorra. Given that their 1–0 victory over Belgium had taken a remarkable amount of mental strength to achieve, now would seem to be a good time to look in more depth at the way Wales had developed such a strong mentality.

The team's mental toughness had been tested on several occasions. There was Gareth Bale's free kick against Andorra. With the win on the line, and nine minutes to go against a team Wales were supposed to wipe the floor with, he had to retake the kick and score from it. That takes something special in psychological terms. So, too, does grabbing four points from two backs-against-the-wall performances against Bosnia and Cyprus. Wales went to Brussels and earned a point against one of the most exciting teams in Europe. They wiped the floor with Israel in their own backyard, and then made the second-best team in the world look ordinary in Cardiff. You can't do this without a massive amount of mental strength – the psychology has to be spot on.

A lot of this derived from Chris Coleman. In his press

conferences Coleman's message to the fans, his players and his coaches had consistently been, 'Listen, we're a good team. We're tough to beat. We're going to go out and make teams earn every pass, every phase of play.' He'd used every minute in front of a microphone or in the presence of a player, a fan or coach, as an opportunity to build that message, giving his players, or anyone who would listen to him, the confidence and belief that Wales could achieve something.

After the Belgium game Coleman had said, as he had after every game, that his staff had been fantastic and they'd worked so hard to gain every 1 per cent in performance. In terms of psychology that 1 per cent can often be the difference. There are plenty of examples in other sports where this has been the case: with Ronnie O'Sullivan and Steve Peters in snooker; Andy Murray and Ivan Lendl in tennis. Lendl might not be a psychologist, but he is someone who knew how to instil belief and a winning mentality in Murray to the point where the Scot finally began to win Grand Slams.

The man tasked with having the same effect on the Wales team, as well as Swansea City, was Ian Mitchell. The first full-time performance psychologist in the Premier League to work in a technical department, Mitchell has a strong playing background, as well as delivering as a coach educator on both UEFA Advanced and Professional licences for the Welsh Football Trust. Before taking on his role with the senior team, Mitchell coached and worked with Wales' under-16s and developed a high-questioning environment at that level, providing insight on how to manage game demands, controlling emotions, motivation and confidence – basic psychological challenges.

The model Mitchell developed worked so well with the under-16s that he was invited by Coleman and Osian Roberts to detail how it might be scaled up to other age groups and eventually the seniors. Mitchell set up a high-performance model similar to the one he'd set up at Swansea City, when the Swans had achieved their best ever points total and finish in the Premier League. The concept was very much bought into by the Welsh set-up and Mitchell was asked to come in and join the senior side for this Euro 2016 qualifying campaign.

In the same way as sports science – which first emerged some 20 years ago – has only readily been taken on board quite recently, the psychological demands of top-level sport are now finally being widely recognised. Mitchell was happy to speak to me about how Wales are working on dealing with that. Here's what he had to say:

JT: What infrastructure was there with regards to Performance Psychology within the Welsh senior team before you took on the job, and has it been a learning curve for you doing this?

IM: I don't think there was someone specifically in my role before me. Coaches and managers will tell you that they've worked psychologically, loosely to a large extent. The danger with that is not what they know but it's what they're missing. Thankfully for me I've done a degree, masters and PhD on this so I understand behaviour. I understand how a group works effectively – that's not saying the coaches don't get that but having someone on board to tighten that up, there's a call for that role. Apparently I'm the first full-time psychologist in the Premier League who works in a technical department. I think my previous playing career helped because I played professionally and was captain of my country at under-18 level. Learning is a big part of it and I've got a strong academic and research background so coming into this environment I think it can be difficult for some people, but I always refer to the importance of contextual intelligence and if you've got that then you can talk in the language of the people you are working with and understand the context of the high performance environment. Every time I talk to a player, I don't refer to research, I do it from a coaching perspective because I know how to do that which helps. It's helped me with players like Ashley Williams and Neil Taylor who play at Swansea. You still have to be accepted, but I'd worked with Neil when he was injured and most of the staff before in coach education, so I think that high level of contextual knowledge has helped me. It isn't an easy environment to work in but it's something that I feel very comfortable in.

JT: How do you bring it all together to pitch to the players? How is it co-ordinated – is it presented to the players as a group, in unit meetings or individually?

IM: We've got a high level of preparation within the camp. I'll meet with Osian and Chris two weeks before and we'll go through everything – how we think the main theme of the camp is and how that consistent message is delivered through meetings and one-on-one meetings with players. Anything to do with what we're going to come up against on the pitch in terms of playing style, such as the physicality or anything that makes you think the other team is going to manage the game differently and it's something that the team has to be weary of, we provide footage of that before the game to show examples. In doing that, there's a psychological message in there that says this could be a highly emotive game so the controlling of their emotions is really important because we obviously need 11 players on the pitch. I don't think it is something that we have to deal with on a one-on-one basis because these are experienced players. They know what to expect and how to use the information we give them. However, if the players come to me and say they need a one-on-one, then I will sit down with them and help them prepare in relation to the tactical information that has been provided throughout the camp. Because I work on the grass with the coaches I understand the message. I understand what is required and my playing and coaching background helps me communicate that to the players. It's a very different approach to your more conventional psychologist, but I work differently and it works in a high-performance environment.

JT: Why do you think it has taken so long for the importance of psychology at the top level of football to be appreciated and taken on board, and how do you approach getting the players on board with it?

IM: I don't think there's a full understanding of the role and what my role is and there's a stigma attached to it that I only talk to players when there's a problem or an issue. If you look at it: technical, tactical, physical and psychological – those are the four pillars of every football game. People say the psychological side of the game is so important but how often do they train that every week? They say it's a huge part but they never work on it. The difficulty of it is that you have great difficulty trying to measure it. You can measure the other aspects, how many successful passes, sprints, how many times they recover position, but with psychology you can't really do that so that's probably why people don't buy into it as much as the other pillars. For me, those four pillars have to be fully integrated into all of the work that you do, so every time you prepare a team you use them. Every time you debrief a team you do the same. It's hidden to a large extent, consciously, because as soon as you say 'we've got a psychology meeting now' we don't want players to get their backs up about it or be fearful of that so we have to integrate it into every piece of work that we do. It's like 20+ years ago when sports science came along, suddenly people were being told they had to train very differently and people didn't like being told how to train, and this is a very similar situation. This sort of role is definitely on the way in now though because people are becoming more aware of it. There are so many psychological demands within the game, with injuries and recovery. It's all part of it, so we have to work a little bit smarter in terms of how we deliver that and getting players to buy in. We've got a lot of players who've worked for 10 to 15 years without it but then I come knocking on the door saying how important it is and these players have been very successful without it, so it's that type of understanding of and sensitivity of how you deliver that message and how you work with players and coaches really, that is key.

JT: What techniques do you teach the players and how are they applied over the course of a training camp?
IM: You're talking about basic psychological skills if you look at it: goal-setting, self-talk, imagery and relaxation are the four basic key skills really and the way you integrate those can effect motivation, confidence, awareness, decision-making, resilience, and the four basic skills are easy to deliver too. With the individual players I work with, I may introduce relaxation techniques which they can use before or

after games but I'm always encouraging them to go through a pre-game routine. The best example to get them to relax would be, 24 hours before the game, when they're cognitively high in terms of thinking about the game, we get them to either physically relax or go through progressive muscular relaxation – where you tense your muscles and release – so you get them to physically relax for about 20 minutes. On top of that, I teach them to use imagery skills in line with the strategies and objectives we've given them technically and tactically. So for example, if we want to press high in the opening five minutes, or sit in a low block because someone is pressing us, each player has different cues and objectives in terms of position and who they're covering. So we get them to relax and picture that in their mind, go through the game, see themselves playing and so on. The third one is to self-talk. Every behaviour is goal-directed and self-talking is really important when you have a switch of focus during a game. If you start to come away from the game-plan and start to do things differently to normal – which comes with pressure, which is natural – self-talk gets you to refocus and get back on process-related information. So it might be as the ball comes over to your side of the pitch you tell yourself where you should be in relation to your nearby players and so on. It's all about verbal cues and triggers, basically, and we get players to practice that in training to take it into a game.

These are basic psychological skills that can be easily applied to individual players but I also work indirectly with the players through the coaches. For example, as the week is periodized physically, I look to shift from motivation at the beginning of the camp to confidence close to a game day. Meetings are arranged early in the week to clarify roles and responsibilities and to provide knowledge on our shape and the opposition. Unit meetings are then arranged to allow ownership and opportunity for the players to discuss any aspects of the game plan. I know that two days before game day is key from a psychological aspect. There is an increase in game anxiety where players will think more frequently and intensely about the game so we lessen the information given to players and look to increase confidence through reflection and pre-game routines. So mental periodization is as important as the physical arrangement of the camp – if you don't acknowledge the psychological demands of the week leading up to the game then you are in danger of players becoming less likely to prepare optimally for the game and probably not being able to function as effectively during the game.

JT: Looking at the Euro 2016 campaign, right from the off the team had a big problem psychologically having to play on a pitch in Andorra that was so bad that some were fearful of being injured on it. How did you combat that?

IM: We got there the day before and I walked out with Chris, had a chat in the middle of the pitch and we just couldn't believe what we were seeing. We knew it was going to be bad, but when we got on it it was 100 times worse really, however it was a conscious decision to play it down before the game and just get on with it. It was definitely on the players' minds, though, that there was a high risk of injury and we knew that but, as mad as it sounds, we tried to minimise distraction as much as possible by not talking about the pitch and the injuries. But we were obviously mindful of it, and that's a classic example of being distracted away from a game plan so we had to reinforce our message of what we were there to do and focus the players on that. Everything about it was a challenge. The place itself, just to get to really, we stayed in Barcelona and travelled from there, it was a beautiful place but it's something that people probably weren't used to in terms of the environment because the stadium was in the middle of houses. It was very tight, very hot, but we just had to manage it as best we could. There was so much to consider that we didn't really know what to expect when we got there, but the Welsh support that night was fantastic. I'll always remember how influential they were mentally for us.

JT: Speaking of fantastic support, the first time the team sampled that crowd, against Bosnia at home, it must have had a massive psychological impact?

IM: It's funny, actually, because I spoke to Chris before and I said I could remember, even before I was involved, that players would walk out onto the pitch before kick-off and the stand opposite the tunnel would be totally empty. How does that impact on a player? It has to have something in there that plays on your motivation. Especially in contrast to when you come out in front of a crowd – in the case of the Bosnia and Cyprus games – that was so electric, it was very different and very special. It was two big games for us, two games that we knew we were up against it with injuries so we talked about resilience a lot, performing under pressure, but the crowd absolutely helped us. It can have the flipside though, especially when you start doing well because there's a certain expectancy there then that you have to live up to and people feel that pressure. We talk a lot in camp about what the expectation is and try to manage that so that we don't become too complacent nor too fuelled. There's a real humbleness in terms of what we're about and what we can achieve but the crowd over those two games was fantastic. The results were huge and it shows the confidence in the squad, there was youth in the side, inexperience in the side, players playing out of position, and it just showed the togetherness in the squad that they were able to pull through and do all of that in the way that they did.

JT: The Belgium away game was a chance to reach a target of hitting eight points after four games – is setting targets a risk if you don't achieve them or achieve them too soon?
IM: It was something that Martyn Margetson [Wales' goalkeeper coach] mentioned and Sam Allardyce was a big advocate of it, looking at the points and what we could expect to achieve so we looked at the average points in terms of the qualifiers in previous years and what you need to do to finish in which position, and that has been a benchmark for us throughout the campaign. The downside of that is if you achieve your goals too soon, because a lot of people will set goals and not readjust them, so I speak to Chris a lot about that. If we reach a goal then we should alter it, just to challenge the group. The performance in Belgium that night, in spite of us knowing how close we were to achieving that target, was incredible in terms of resiliency because we defended so well and could have nicked it at the end. For us to achieve those points in that time-frame was challenging for us but very realistic, we felt, which just shows the

confidence of the group really in terms of the staff and what we knew we were capable of.

JT: Some strong messages have been conveyed from the press conferences in this campaign too – how extensively is that coordinated in terms of the message you want to convey, particularly away to Israel?

IM: Absolutely. I work very closely with Chris anyway, but press conferences are a big part that I've put a lot of effort into in terms of the major themes we want to put out. I sit in on all of the press conferences anyway and give feedback to Chris and Ashley afterwards but you've got to remember with a press conference that you're not just talking to the press, you're talking to the fans, players, everyone, because of social media nowadays everyone has access to it so we always try and go into them with clear messages that we want to disseminate. In light of how tough we built the game up to be, and in light of the result, they didn't necessarily reflect each other, but I think when it comes to keeping ourselves grounded in the wake of that, it always comes back to that underdog mentality that we have. If you're successful, complacency isn't far behind, you're at your most vulnerable when you're successful. As for the trip itself, it was a hot place obviously, hostile atmosphere in the game, not the easiest place to get to, but when we arrived we went out into the press conference and told them how tough this game was going to be. We didn't want to say it was just something we'd want to just get something out of, we wanted to build up how close the two sides were, how difficult a place it was to go to and how strong they were. We knew if we flipped the expectations and painted ourselves as the underdogs then the guys would react better to that so we wanted to show them it was going to be a tough game.

I actually sat down and planned the key message, as it was highly possible that the game was perceived to be a high-pressure game. I know pressure has the ability to disrupt things that we value as a team so it was important that we focused on minimising anything that added to the perception of pressure. Playing down the outcome of games has been a key message that I worked on with Chris. It's always about the process (i.e. the performance) and not the outcome (i.e. the result). For this particular camp it was important for us to enhance confidence as often as possible, both on and off the grass. I spoke a lot about maintaining optimism and managing expectation – the vocabulary we used in meetings, focusing on the things that were in our control, providing opportunities to tap into the motivation of the players and staff and to explain the 'why' of everything we do in order to empower the players and strengthen our identity.

JT: How integral have Chris Coleman and Ashley Williams been to disseminating those messages in press conferences?

IM: I think you've got to take your hat off to Chris and Ashley in terms of their leadership really, because it's about representing the true values of the group and with Ashley and Chris we have two leaders who are very believable and very trustworthy and the players buy into that. They've played a big role in that resilience, that toughness of the group, they know exactly what they can do and what they can't do. There's a real level-headedness in terms of expectation and what they're there to do. Chris has said several times that he can see so much of himself in Ashley and, if you look at the two of them, Ashley doesn't miss many games, he's Mr Consistency, will roll his sleeves up, he's very tough, and Chris was exactly the same as the player. I think Ashley would see himself within Chris as well, there's a respect that he wouldn't address him as a player but he sees a lot of the player still in Chris, so Ashley has bought into that side of his manager and so have the other players. There are a lot of similarities between the two and they have played a massive role in all of this. They both demonstrate transformational leadership characteristics in that they understand Wales' international culture, their actions reflect the values of the squad, and they are seen to deliver what matters to the players, fans and the nation as a whole.

JT: As this campaign has progressed, the confidence has grown in all quarters. You can see signs of that in Chris Coleman too, but given what he's been through with Wales he has the right to show that confidence doesn't he?

IM: Given what he had to deal with, absolutely. The transition that Chris has been involved with since becoming the manager of the Wales team was something that was obviously extremely difficult to take over. Something he's always wanted to do though, you know. You're right, you're going to have very difficult moments as a manager, none more so than what he did, but you can see a very confident manager there at the moment and rightly so. The team are very confident, and we've earned that right to be confident. That's not being cocky, we've earned that right because we've matched up against some of the best sides in the world, and beaten them on occasions. But we're still learning, I'm still learning. Chris is, too, even though he's got a wealth of experience as a manager, he'll tell you that, but we've got a very good group so there is a right to be confident. I think Chris' passion is really visible for everyone to see. We're a nation who have to do well as a group. Coaches coming into Wales and working in Wales realise we're a nation who work as a group and Chris recognises that but that passion that he brings into the process is something that is really easy for the players and the fans to pick up on, and I think a lot of our momentum has come from what Chris has brought in in that regard.

JT: In terms of that performance against Belgium, is that a culmination of everything that you've been working on in the campaign so far? The various systems that were used, the strong mentality, the never-say-die attitude, it was all there.
IM: The big word for me is adaptability, the better teams can adapt to various systems. These systems aren't just flipped in the game every now and then, there's a conscious effort in training to work on these formations as much as we can, we give the players cues and triggers in terms of positional information and formation so it is very clear, if we have to change in the middle of a game, what everyone needs to do. I think that has been a major strength, Chris has shown that he is at the highest level tactically. If we'd stuck to one system in some of the games we've played in this campaign though then we quite conceivably could have come unstuck so it's a credit to the team that we've been so adaptable. The grittiness of the performance against Belgium at home was the most pleasing thing for me: [Chris] Gunter

out of position, Jazz [Richards] was coming in for his campaign debut, James [Chester] had just been relegated with Hull, there were different situations within that game but the maturity in that group and the way they handled everything was second to none and again it shows how far the squad has come.

Talking to Ian Mitchell, it surprised me how thorough the behind-the-scenes processes are. Not that the set-up isn't thorough in the way it does things, of course it is. We've seen examples of that so often in other fields, such as, when was the last time a player was injured on Wales duty? It certainly isn't as frequent as it used to be. It was just somewhat surprising that so much work goes into the press conferences, that so much work is done on reinforcing the goals of any given training camp at any given point within a training camp, that managing the mentality isn't just something Chris Coleman likes to control from the top table of press conferences, but something that is thought about and designed relentlessly behind the scenes. It all adds up and it has all been of massive benefit to the team so far in this campaign, but with Wales now leading the group, a new psychological challenge would present itself going into the remainder of the campaign – dealing with having a target on their back.

CHAPTER 14

Cyprus vs Wales / Wales vs Israel – 3 / 6 September 2015

'We haven't qualified yet, we've got a lot of work to do and big performances to come. If this group of players are the best we've had, then we've got to go there and get a result.'

CHRIS COLEMAN, WALES MANAGER

FOLLOWING THE AWAY game against Belgium, Mark Pitman said that the pressure of expectation would be on Chris Coleman's men from that point forward. Who'd have thought that ten months later Wales would be in the position they found themselves in going into these two games against Cyprus and Israel? Top of the group following a 3–0 demolition of Israel in Haifa and a historic 1–0 win against Belgium in Cardiff – the results couldn't have gone better with six points from six. But the manner of the performances were what really seemed to give people optimism going into these next two games.

Everybody wanted to think about France; people were booking trips already, although to be fair some people had been doing that since the Israel away game, and with the possibility of securing qualification early if Wales won these next two games, the prospect of reaching the finals of a major tournament was almost too close for people to control themselves. 'I don't think you'd be human if you didn't dream about reaching France,' said James Chester in the build-up to the game. 'We've given ourselves a great chance. There are only four games left and, having a five-point gap between ourselves and third, I think it's a real possibility that we'll manage to do that. It is important that we stay focused on the games that we've got, games that are very winnable, but I think if we don't qualify from the position we're in now then we'll struggle to live it down.' No pressure, then.

Even the World Cup draw in July couldn't distract Chris Coleman, despite the manager being asked all sorts of questions about Wales by the international press. You can understand the situation, such a remarkable turnaround, top ten in the world for the first time, top seeds for the first time. But, regardless of drawing Serbia in their group, which was significant because the 6–1 defeat to Serbia back in 2012 had been when everyone seemed to believe that Chris Coleman had started to take control of his Wales future, utter focus on Cyprus was demonstrated. Even amid talk of a new contract for the man in charge, Coleman was unwavering in his focus on the task at hand. When pressed at the squad announcement for these two games regarding his contract situation, Coleman was holistic in his response. 'We all went out for food after the draw in Russia,' said the manager, 'myself, and the delegation that came over to Russia, such as the FAW President, the CEO and so on, and we had an informal chat. My reason for not getting into all of this is simple: we haven't got the job done yet and we need to get to France. If we achieve that target – and I've believed for a long time that we will do it in this campaign because of the depth, talent and experience we have in the squad – then fine, we'll sit down and have that discussion about a new contract or an extension, but until then we're not going into it.'

Not one person referenced in this book would ever dispute Chris Coleman's passion for Wales; even in the aftermath of the tragic passing of his close friend Gary Speed, Chris Coleman's passion was unquestionable. The results were tough, yes, but whether that was the case or not then his passion for the cause was, and still very much is, indisputable; anyone who has ever watched him on the touchline or in a press conference can attest to that. It speaks volumes that, in a squad announcement where some real concerns were brought up, such as Wales' lack of holding midfielders with Joe Allen, David Vaughan and others out, as well as the totally different challenge that Cyprus would pose on their own turf, the one thing that the fans picked out on social media in the days to follow was Coleman's show of passion for the job. 'Even throughout the last campaign, when we all had such a horrible time following Gary's passing, managing my country was then, and still is, the biggest job there is in football to me,' insisted Coleman, 'and the biggest honour that could possibly be bestowed upon me in my career – regardless of whether it is a successful tenure or not. I don't want that honour to be taken away from me, of course I don't, but I still want to finish this current campaign on a successful note by reaching France and we can only do that by concentrating on each game in turn. The next campaign will be here soon enough but this campaign is obviously the priority at the moment. The pressure is enormous, but this time in my career right now stands out as the biggest challenge and honour that I have ever had in my life.'

There were some real issues to worry about going into these games, but Coleman's passion seemed to reassure the fans that Wales were capable of getting the job done. It was an incredible thing to say, really, considering just twelve months before there had been people calling for him to be sacked following the Andorra away game. The FIFA world rankings would help aid people's confidence, too, of course, as Wales would maintain their position of ninth best team in the world. England would slip below them into tenth, meaning Wales would be ranked above them for the first time ever – something that gave the fans immense pleasure for obvious reasons.

Newly-promoted assistant manager Osian Roberts was typically measured looking ahead to the prospect of playing Cyprus, as he stressed that Wales would not be getting carried away in spite of their recent victory over Belgium. 'For us, carrying on to concentrate on our performances and improving every area of our play is the target,' said Roberts. 'We cannot afford to rest on our laurels because of what we did against

Belgium, we always have to ask more of ourselves. Reflecting is a big part of the process after every game, as it gives us an opportunity to assess what we did well and what we need to work on, and that leads us onwards. A lot of work has been done in that regard behind the scenes already of course and, although we play Israel so soon after Cyprus, Cyprus is our single focus and we have to get everything ready to face them, because we're aware of what is possible for us in the next few games with regards to qualification and putting in the best possible performance against Cyprus is key to that.'

Wales captain Ashley Williams stopped just shy of saying that he'd banned his teammates from looking ahead to Israel in the pre-match press conference. 'I refuse to look at Israel or the other two games,' he said, 'and I won't let the boys do it either. We're just so focused on this game because we understand how big it is. It's three important points to play for and we don't want to give those up – it would be silly to be thinking about Israel, Bosnia or Andorra, this game is too big and Cyprus are good so if we don't focus on them we'll get hurt.'

So the job of managing the mind-set seemed well in hand, as focus and concentration and not getting ahead of themselves were key themes in the Wales media sessions before the game. Wales' team hotel was littered with Together Stronger posters yet again, too, to keep everyone focused. This particular batch read: 'Together we stand on the brink of history.' The whole set-up knew how close they were, but the message was very much to continue doing what they'd been doing, and keep working hard to push themselves across the line.

Both teams would have especially tight time constraints to work in because, as it had been earlier in the campaign when Wales played Bosnia and Cyprus at home, the first game took place just four days after the squad had been on club duty, with the second game played three days after that – two games and all of the preparation that goes into it in the space of seven days. This was in stark contrast to Belgium in the previous game. Because it had been played in the off-season Wales had

had two weeks to prepare for one game. And during the two international windows prior to that Wales had had a whole week to prepare for one game.

Although the injuries to Joe Allen and David Vaughan were big losses to the squad, it was clear Joe Ledley could comfortably play the more combative holding role, freeing up Andy King or David Edwards to play a role similar to Joe Allen's, even if they weren't the type of players that would usually play Allen's more dictatorial role. But Ledley was a booking away from suspension and playing against such a combative side like Cyprus raised concerns that the midfielder could quite easily get booked and miss the second game against Israel, thus potentially leaving Wales even shorter for numbers in the middle. The calling up of young Liverpool midfielder Jordan Williams pleased many, a very highly-rated teenager who fans had been talking up for some time, but whether or not he could handle that stage, especially if called upon against Israel where Wales could qualify if things went their way against Cyprus, was a question everyone wanted answering. Coleman explained the logic behind his decision. 'We know these two games are going to be two more high pressure games of football and Jordan's played at Anfield,' said Coleman. 'There's pressure every game for Liverpool and that's why we went down that route.'

The injury situation was exacerbated in the days building up to the game, with Hal Robson-Kanu and James Chester both suffering knocks while on club duty just days before the Wales fixtures took place. Robson-Kanu would start for Wales against Cyprus, James Chester would miss out, but the biggest injury blow was confirmed just hours before kick-off as Joe Ledley pulled out with a hamstring injury and would likely miss both games – an enormous blow as the axis of the team had been wiped out by injury. It meant a David Edwards / Andy King combination would occupy the middle of the park. Chris Coleman had spoken in his pre-match press conference of how lucky Wales had been in some respects regarding their injuries, because if Chester was out then the very experienced

James Collins could step in or Chris Gunter could move inside to central defence and Jazz Richards could play at right-back. It was the same for Hal Robson-Kanu, as Sam Vokes or Simon Church could come in there, but in central midfield it was a bit more difficult given how specific the roles of Allen and Ledley were.

Emyr Huws could fill Allen's role, but he was a long-term absentee and wasn't in this squad. David Vaughan could do Ledley's role but was missing, too. Although there was no real concern from the fans, who were all pretty much on cloud nine, it would be fair to say that perhaps neither David Edwards nor Andy King were totally suited to the holding roles that they would have to play in this game. Nonetheless, those were the roles they were selected to fill, as Wales went for what was becoming their default set-up of playing three at the back. Hennessey started in goal; his turn to win his 50th cap. Chris Gunter, Ashley Williams and Ben Davies played ahead of him, with Jazz Richards and Neil Taylor filling the wing-back slots. Andy King and David Edwards occupied the central roles. Aaron Ramsey played just ahead of them as a 10, with Gareth Bale and Hal Robson-Kanu leading the line.

Yet again, thousands of Welsh fans made the trip out to support their men in their quest to qualify for a tournament. Nicosia was pretty dead in the days leading up to the game, as most fans – 4,000 of them to be precise – were camped out in the resorts like Ayia Napa before heading to the capital on the afternoon of the game to quite literally paint the town red with their sunburn and their Wales tops. Over 40 coach loads of Wales fans made their way into Nicosia that night, making their presence known the minute they got to the stadium, drowning out the noise of the Cypriots and their drums for the entirety of the evening. The Welsh fans also paid tribute to one of their own, a young Wales fan named Gareth Seville, who had sadly passed away in the weeks building up to the game. It speaks volumes for the level of Welsh support in this game that, afterwards, a number of Chris Coleman's players were remarking on how the atmosphere had felt more like that of a home game than an away game for them.

It had never been this hot at a Wales home game though, that's for sure, and, as well as Wales started, the heat was definitely a problem. A breathless opening 15 minutes saw Wales settle into their stride, Ramsey and Bale in particular making a nuisance of themselves while evading some pretty strong challenges, and creating some good chances. Cyprus' game-plan at that point – and throughout the game, to be honest – was obvious. They simply tried to play lofted passes in behind the Wales defence for their number nine to run on to and give Ashley Williams something to think about. Ramsey came very close to opening the scoring for Wales from a counterattack inside the opening ten minutes, which culminated with a curling effort being struck wide from outside the box. But Wales' best chance of the opening exchanges came from a Gareth Bale free kick. The Cypriot goalkeeper couldn't get a grip on a typically dipping and weaving ball and spilled it into the way of Neil Taylor. One-on-one with the goalkeeper, the left-back could only hit his shot straight at the stopper, who saved comfortably.

If ever there was an example of how restless the Wales fans were about winning this game, it came in the first half as Bale found some space out on the right flank before crossing in for Edwards to head the ball into the back of the net. There was absolute hysteria from the Wales fans for about a second, until the referee blew his whistle to penalise Robson-Kanu for a foul off the ball and rule out the goal. This was greeted by a collective groan that sounded more like a thunderstorm than a show of anxiety. But the Welsh fans, players and journalists were anxious – and those few seconds were a very powerful example of that.

After this, the game got away from Wales, as without Joe Allen in the middle to dictate the tempo of their play, Coleman's men were playing at a demanding pace without any respite, which saw the performance level slip slightly as a result. While the Cypriots were physical, and tackling pretty hard throughout the first half in particular, their general energy was very impressive. They were closing down the Welsh at a blistering pace and forcing them to think twice about playing their default way of passing in favour of a more mid-range approach where they weren't just looking for the closest pass, but the one that could spread the pitch a bit more. Coleman could frequently be seen gesturing from the touchline for more width from his team.

Half-time brought little change, as the second half was a frustrating affair for the most-part for Wales. The final ball was still missing, Aaron Ramsey was having a pretty torrid time trying to link up the play from a fairly deep-sitting midfield duo to the forwards, and wasn't having much luck in finding the wing-backs either to aid his efforts. Ramsey would get a bit of criticism for his performance in this game, losing the ball eight times in the first half alone, but on the flip-side this showed he was trying to make things happen. It just wasn't falling right for him.

Wales were doing very well at the back, though. Ashley Williams would again be most people's shout for Man of the Match after his performance, but Jazz Richards and Neil Taylor were excellent again in trying to get things going down the flanks, even if it didn't come to anything very often, and they were well protected by the midfield duo they had in front of them in David Edwards and Andy King. While Osian Roberts labelled the fact that King and Edwards were able to come in and do such a good job as one of 'the secrets to the team's success', Ashley Williams would be equally complimentary after the game. 'Kingy and Dave Edwards were unbelievable tonight, coming in as attack-minded players and sitting in those holding roles doing the job defensively,' Williams would say. 'It's a strength of ours that whoever is in our squad, we don't think about who's missing because when the people that come in do that good a job it doesn't matter too much.'

Offensively Wales were quite pedestrian, though, as evidenced by the fact that it took until the 71st minute for

Wales to make any real attack of note in the second half, a cutback from Bale to substitute Sam Vokes which couldn't find its way cleanly to Vokes' feet, nor the target. The fans were getting restless. They were still bellowing chants of support from behind Hennessey's goal but you could sense the anxiety creeping in. The clock was running down and, although Wales clearly hadn't played to their best up to this point in the game, the score-line didn't look like changing any time soon.

Cue the Ramsey and Bale show. Neither had managed to have much of an impact on the game after that initial opening flurry of chances, but they both found their feet again going into the closing stages of the game. Ramsey in particular was instigating all sorts of great moves, cut-backs, one-twos, anything to try and find the crucial opening. It soon came, with Ramsey again at the heart of the play when he fed an overlapping Jazz Richards with a neat flick, after seemingly being penned in on the touchline by two defenders. The wing-back curled an incredibly inviting cross towards the far post, where the most expensive player in the world would again rise up to prove how invaluable he was to Wales. Bale towered over the Cypriot defence to rifle a header into the back of the net with less than ten minutes to go.

Of the nine goals Wales had scored in this qualifying campaign, Gareth Bale had assisted or scored eight of them up to this point. Each one had seemed more important than the last, as was evidenced when Wales' number 11 ran over to the dugout to celebrate with all of the coaches and the subs. Together Stronger – there were many moments throughout this campaign that embodied those words, but this one was iconic. To see the elation on every single member of the playing and coaching staff's faces, as Bale ran over to them to celebrate to the soundtrack of 4,000 Welsh fans going absolutely berserk, was proof of the togetherness and team spirit that had developed within Welsh football. Now 1–0 up, with less than ten minutes to go, everyone knew how close Wales were to victory and, despite a few moments where Cyprus threw everything at Wales in an effort to push for the draw, Ashley Williams and his defensive partners saw Wales through to full-time with their lead intact. It hadn't been pretty by any stretch, but Wales had done it.

Having secured the win, and shut the door on the opposition strikers for another 90 minutes, Wales recorded a fourth clean sheet in a row for the first time since 1981. Their record of not conceding a goal in open play throughout qualifying had continued for another game thanks to another spectacular defensive effort from Wales. Inevitably, with Bale getting the winner, sceptics would bring up the 'one-man team' rubbish again about Wales. This was a naïve assessment. The fact was that Wales had kept five clean sheets in qualifying up to this point and that had been down to the entire team, if not specifically the defenders.

Ashley Williams felt the defensive effort from his teammates had been 'unbelievable'. 'We work very hard on the defensive end of our play,' said the skipper, 'and you can see the desire in everyone to stop crosses, to block shots, to stay with runners, all the dirty little bits, and some people don't notice the boys are doing it so well. It's very nice to get another clean sheet away from home. We feel if we keep a clean sheet then, more often than not, we're going to win the game.'

Assistant manager Osian Roberts concurred, adding that it was inevitable that Ramsey and Bale could not be kept quiet for the whole 90 minutes. 'We knew that as long as we could stay in it these players can just spark out of nowhere and combine to create a match-winning goal against any team,' said Roberts. 'Fortunately tonight that has happened once again. There is always going to be a spell in the game where one or both of them find space a bit easier or do something really special, which makes it nigh-on impossible for teams to deal with them properly. That is the talent that they have. That's why they're so special.'

It had been a very difficult game for Wales on the whole, given the heat, the injuries and the playing surface which wasn't great, but no-one really wanted to complain about it given what they'd gone through in Andorra. They'd done exceptionally well to get their first win in Cyprus for 23 years. Israel would present a totally different challenge, as expectations went into total overdrive for this game, from a fan's perspective at least. When the word 'destiny' is being thrown about, you know expectations don't get much higher. There was a nice symmetry to it. When Wales had qualified for their last major tournament in 1958, they'd done it against Israel and beat them in Cardiff to seal it.

Israel's manager Eli Guttman was very confident in his press conferences building up to the game, alluding to a masterplan that he had to 'ensure Wales wouldn't be celebrating qualification after the game. Wales are a very successful team,' said Guttman. 'They focus on each game in turn but we're ready. We took Andorra seriously in our last game and we're doing the same with this game. We ignore Wales' position, we focus on our game and leave the thought of qualification to the Welsh people. I don't think that we weren't ready last time we played them, but we have used that experience to prepare for this game. We're focused, we're ready, wanting to play the game. It is very important to get points from tomorrow, if we do what we trained for then we can get points for sure.'

Guttman's confidence was interesting to see, not because it was unexpected but because, when speaking to the Israeli journalists afterwards, it was clear that some of them couldn't work out what he was up to. He clearly had a plan, but what was that plan? No-one really knew what to expect. The only thing the Israeli media seemed certain of was that there would be three central midfielders – Nir Bitton, Beram Kayal and Bebras Natcho. Only the latter had featured in Guttman's starting XI in Haifa in the reverse fixture. With Guttman saying they'd learnt their lessons from Haifa, a very physical approach from Israel seemed to be on the cards. Selecting three physical, industrious central midfielders in the team suggested Wales were in for a very tough game in front of their home fans in Cardiff, just three days after labouring to their victory over Cyprus. Sure enough, when the teams were released, Israel had opted to take a leaf out of Wales' book and go with three centre-backs; a 5–3–2. All-out defence seemed to be the plan, as there was no playmaker in the Israel side. The three midfielders were fairly defensive-minded. Eran Zahavi was the biggest threat, but playing up front with no-one to feed him suggested it was going to be a very defensive Israel that tried to play on the counter.

Despite being only 90 minutes away from accomplishing arguably the biggest feat in Welsh football history, again there was a distinct lack of tension inside the Cardiff City Stadium. I'll spare them from the embarrassment of naming them but, before the game, as thousands of fans were bopping around to Zombie Nation, a couple of guys in the media section were clearly enjoying it too. It definitely didn't feel like a game of the magnitude that it was.

Much more fluent than they had been in Nicosia, Wales set to work on breaking down Israel's defensive set-up from the moment they got possession. There was no dilly-dallying, they just went for it. Targeting the left side of Israel's defence, somewhere Guttman's team particularly struggled and apparently a big factor in why the Israel manager had chosen to put an extra man in at the back, Wales found good fortune with Ramsey, King, Edwards and Robson-Kanu all having efforts on the Israel goal. From a Welsh perspective, the only thing that was missing from the opening exchanges was a goal. Everything else was going as well as anyone could have expected it to, so much so that some of Israel's players – Zahavi in particular – could be seen complaining to their manager about the defensive system. But Guttman stuck with it.

What Wales were up against here was a totally new challenge. They'd played against defensive teams before. They themselves had played very defensively against a very good attacking team before. But it had been a very long time since they'd last played a team that deliberately set out to get a draw and nothing else against them. It's a consequence of being ranked as one of the top teams in the world, and not being beaten competitively for nearly two years, that teams aren't going to come to you any more and let you have your way. They're going to make you work hard for it, exactly like Israel were doing to Wales in this game.

Wales were dominating everything: chance creation, possession, territory, the midfield battle, everything but the score-line. They just couldn't get the decisive goal. Thunderous applause greeted every time Wales were rewarded with a set-piece, or broke into the final third, such was the anticipation that this decisive goal was going to come. But Israel remained resolute throughout. Andy King went the closest after connecting with a Ramsey corner. It was one of those where the crowd was celebrating the second it left King's head, as he seemingly couldn't miss, but the keeper got across excellently to deny the effort. Hal Robson-Kanu had what looked like a stonewall penalty appeal denied as well. Nothing was dropping for Wales. It was just one of those games, but they kept plugging away.

It felt like every other play ended up in Wales getting into a really dangerous position, or getting a shot away; Bale, Ramsey, Dave Edwards, they were all having a pop at it but none of them could get through. By the time the game reached its closing stages, Wales had Bale, Ramsey, Sam Vokes and Simon Church all on the pitch at the same time, such was the desperation to get the decisive goal and land the victory that would guarantee the Red Dragons' passage to France – which, in all fairness, they deserved after the dominance they'd displayed, but it just wouldn't materialise. Church had the ball in the back of the net for Wales with practically the last touch of the game, but it was rightly ruled out for offside. Guttman had been proven right, Wales weren't going to leave the Cardiff City Stadium celebrating that night as the game would finish 0–0.

Trying to think of the right words to sum up that performance is difficult, because Wales played very, very well. Fate wanted to make them wait, it would seem. 'It was a little bit of an anticlimax,' admitted Ben Davies. 'We were confident enough that we could beat them. On the night we played well enough, dominated the game and we probably should have got the win but at the end of the day we didn't and you have to look at it as a point gained. We'd have taken this scenario at the start of the group, eight games in and only needing one more point to qualify, so we can't complain too much.'

In reality, Chris Coleman's men had to take the opposition's performance as a compliment. They'd improved to such a point that teams were having to come and play against them and change their style dramatically. Israel were a good team in front of goal, but they sacrificed all of that to ensure Wales wouldn't have an easy win. 'As we become more and more successful we'll need to learn to deal with this,' said Aaron Ramsey. 'Teams are going to do this against us. We will have to be more clinical in front of goal and take more of our chances – something we missed tonight, which is disappointing. We've learnt from this game too, we've shown a lot of patience to keep possession but we need to learn when to move the ball quicker, know the importance of opening that gap up and then show the ability to take advantage of that. If we can do all of that, then games like this are going to open up for us and it'll be a lot easier.'

It wasn't as if there was a sense of doom and gloom in the mixed zone after the game, but there were a few wry smiles because this had been a chance, a really solid opportunity for Wales to break their qualification hoodoo. Having come so close to pulling it off, it was a bit of a disappointment that everyone was going to have to wait another month for another opportunity. Cyprus could conceivably have aided Chris Coleman's men by holding Belgium to a draw in the late kick-off of the day, but Belgium scored in the last few minutes after putting in an indifferent performance throughout the rest of the game. It just wasn't meant to happen at that particular moment.

A month would feel like such a long time, but, as most pointed out, Wales had waited nearly 60 years to qualify for another tournament, and had found themselves after this round of fixtures within a point of achieving that. Waiting another month to see what happened against Bosnia and Andorra wasn't going to be that difficult – was it?

Standings after Matchdays 7 & 8

Pos.	Team	GP	W	D	L	F	A	GD	Pts
1	Wales	8	5	3	0	9	2	7	18
2	Belgium	8	5	2	1	17	3	14	17
3	Israel	8	4	1	3	14	9	5	13
4	Bosnia	8	3	2	3	12	10	2	11
5	Cyprus	8	3	0	5	12	13	- 1	9
6	Andorra	8	0	0	8	3	30	- 27	0

Matchday 7 results:

Cyprus 0–1 Wales
Belgium 3–1 Bosnia & Herzegovina
Israel 4–0 Andorra

Matchday 8 results:

Wales 0–0 Israel
Bosnia & Herzegovina 3–0 Andorra
Cyprus 0–1 Belgium

CHAPTER 15

Bosnia vs Wales / Wales vs Andorra – 10 / 13 October 2015

'I've never had a feeling like this. When you achieve this,
it's the holy grail for us really, we've been chasing it for
long enough. You never spell Wales with a Q do you?'

CHRIS COLEMAN, WALES MANAGER

'THE FULL-TIME WHISTLE has gone in Jerusalem. Israel are
beaten by Cyprus. Wales have qualified. Three words a nation
thought it might never hear again.' Those were the words
broadcast by Sky Sports after the full-time whistle in the
Bosnian city of Zenica. It was true that they were words a
nation thought it might never hear again, but now that it had
heard them, they wouldn't be forgotten in a hurry.

In the days building up to that massive game in Bosnia,
a small, vociferous band of about 700 Welsh fans had made
the testing trip to eastern Europe to witness the moment for
which most of them had waited a lifetime. You know it's been
an incredibly long time since Wales last qualified for a major
tournament when you can confidently say that most of the fan-
base wasn't alive at the time or old enough to remember it.
In 1958 Wales had qualified for the World Cup in Sweden in
unusual circumstances; this time it was conventional, no play-
offs, no drawing straws to see who would play the team no-one
else wanted to play. Wales had done it and the delirium back
home, and in a soaking wet corner of a stadium in Zenica, was
beautiful.

Despite being on the cusp of making history, during the

build-up to this momentous occasion the Wales players displayed the mental stability that had become a mainstay during this campaign. That said, you could just sense that the magnitude of the achievement in front of them was starting to enter their minds. But who could blame them? Prior to the Bosnia game, Chris Gunter admitted that the prospect of what was to come had entered his mind, but he insisted the team would remain focused. 'It's no different for us,' he said. 'When we meet up we do the same thing every time, whether we're top of the group or bottom. We're preparing exactly the same way. We're not thinking about anything other than Saturday – we never think about the second game in these windows where there's two games. It's been a campaign full of highs and hopefully there is one more major high to come and we want to let the fans dream about what's coming. But up until then you can't let your mind wander, we just need to get the job done and see what happens.'

Chris Coleman on the other hand, while conveying his usual calmness when announcing the squad, spoke very buoyantly at the FAW Awards dinner five days before the game, declaring that Wales would qualify for Euro 2016. It was the first time he had done so in public. With the greatest respect to the two teams Wales faced in this window, with just one point required for qualification if Israel won both of their games (at home to Cyprus and away to Belgium), Coleman's defiance was hardly a sign of over-confidence. After what Wales had already achieved in this group, to expect a point from an away game against Bosnia or a home game against Andorra wasn't unreasonable. From day one in this group this squad of Welsh players had developed a reputation for leaving absolutely everything on the pitch. So to expect anything less than 100 per cent effort and dedication from the squad to the task of getting six points from these next two fixtures was foolhardy.

In spite of his bullishness regarding Wales' qualification chances, on the verge of his biggest success as Wales manager, Coleman reflected on his biggest failing – the 6–1 mauling his team suffered at the hands of Serbia in Novi Sad. 'I had doubts whether I was capable of doing the job after the Serbia game,' Coleman revealed. 'We didn't just lose, we embarrassed ourselves and when you do that you embarrass the country – and that's another ball game. I'd never felt that before. But I think I'd have been a bit of a coward if I'd walked away. If it is a fight, my father always said to me: "If you lose, you've got to be walking forward throwing punches back, not on your hands and knees crawling away getting kicked in the backside."'

Fittingly enough, the match in Zenica would be the closest Wales had been geographically to Novi Sad since that night in 2012, meaning Chris Coleman's Wales tenure would be coming full circle in a sense, from that devastating defeat to this, the night Wales made history. The mood in Serbia three years previously had been one of overwhelming misery, but the boot would be firmly on the other foot in Bosnia. And yet, anyone who thought Wales would beat Bosnia comfortably, and walk off into the sunset having qualified for the Euros that way, had another thing coming. This was Wales, and if this book has taught you anything so far then it's that here in Wales we don't do anything the easy way when it comes to football. And so it proved in Zenica.

It was never going to be the best of games. The weather in the city was so bad in the hours leading up to the game and so much was at stake for both teams. Bosnia needed a win to keep their play-off hopes alive and Wales wanted to better or equal Israel's result in order to avoid a nervy last game against Andorra in Cardiff. There was a very raucous atmosphere at the Stadion Bolino Polje in Zenica, created by both sets of fans. It was almost a battle against the elements, if you like – the weather, the crowd, the opposition, the occasion. If Wales' dragons were going to qualify in this game, then what a night to do it.

Wales named a full-strength side of Hennessey; Gunter, Williams, Davies; Richards, Ledley, Allen, Taylor; Bale, Ramsey and Robson-Kanu. Bosnia on the other hand were without key players like Džeko and Bešić. With the former on the bench and the latter suspended, you could say Bosnia were like a wounded animal in this fixture, and they proved the old saying true. Wounded animals are more dangerous. Miralem Pjanić, Wales' nemesis from the reverse fixture, proved himself to be one of the most underrated attacking players in world football, as he persistently found pockets of space in the midst of a very tight Welsh backline that hadn't conceded a goal from open play in eight games. A cagey first half with few clear-cut chances saw Wales labour to half-time with the scores even. They'd been unfortunate not to take the lead after their own number 10, Aaron Ramsey, had jinked his way into the box after a lay-off by Robson-Kanu, dummied two defenders on the edge of the six-yard box and squared for Taylor, but his attempt was scuppered excellently by Begović.

After getting the job done in the first half, coming through it with the point they needed intact, it always felt like it was going to be squeaky bum time for Wales in the second half – from this fan's perspective anyway. Wales had been in good positions to qualify so many times in previous years and it had fallen apart for one reason or another. Sod's Law surely decreed it was going to happen here, or the celebrations were at least going to be delayed again, as they had been a month ago with the draw against Israel.

Bosnia certainly tried their best to make that happen as, apart from a Bale effort from the left side of the box that swerved wide of the near post, Pjanić and his teammates were looking every inch as dangerous as Wales were. The introduction of Milan Djurić – a 6ft 6in, mobile centre-forward – certainly seemed to swing things in Bosnia's favour. As well as Pjanić's dexterity in terms of his short passing game, Bosnia had a big target for him to feed now too. Sure enough, ten minutes later the two combined to put Bosnia ahead. A long diagonal free kick was allowed to bounce in Wales' box, after Ashley Williams and Vedad Ibišević both missed the initial delivery, which gave Djurić the perfect angle to direct a lofted header over Hennessey. Wales were behind for the first time since the opening group game against Andorra 13 months before.

There was no panic from the Welsh faithful, though, they kept singing their songs, chanting away because at the Teddy Stadium in Jerusalem, Cyprus were winning against Israel, and either way Wales were through. But the mood changed just five minutes later when news came through of an Israel equaliser. Suddenly Wales fans were looking over their shoulders. Not again. Surely not this time, not after everything the team had been through in the past few years to get to this point? Of course, if Israel won against Cyprus, then Wales still had the Andorra home game from which to get the point they needed. But that game was meant to be a big party, a chance to celebrate the momentous achievement that was hopefully going to be confirmed in Zenica on this bitter October evening. It wasn't supposed to be a nervy affair, where Wales would have one desperate last chance to earn a point against a team who would surely park the bus and play on the counter.

Then it happened. For the first time in generations – after Joe Jordan, after Romania in 1993, after the collapse in 2004 qualifying, after everything that had conspired against Wales' dream to reach the pinnacle of football again after 1958, luck finally went Wales' way when it mattered. In Jerusalem, Cyprus retook the lead against Israel with ten minutes to go. It was quite a sight to see 700 people jumping up and down and cheering in a frenzy, celebrating a goal they hadn't witnessed, scored by a player most of them had probably never heard of. There were 700 roaring dragons penned into a tiny corner of this old, wet stadium in Bosnia, but the ecstasy that was soon to follow would warm the souls of an entire nation.

Bosnia went on to score again to put Wales 2–0 down but nobody Welsh cared. If you'd asked any Welshman there in Zenica who had scored that goal, then none of them would have been able to tell you. It was totally irrelevant. They were all glued to their phones, checking to see what was happening in Jerusalem, where Cyprus were giving Wales the breathing space they needed to secure their passage to France.

After all the adversity of this campaign, with injuries, suspensions and some bad luck; after the adversity Wales had endured in the previous 58 years of trying to get back to the apex of international football, fortune had found Wales again. With the full-time whistle blown in Zenica and in Jerusalem, Wales had finally returned to football's promised land – the finals of a European Championship tournament. Those three words a nation thought it might never hear again – 'Wales have qualified'.

Surreal, ecstatic, berserk, just plain insane – I don't know how you'd describe the atmosphere in the ground after that game. The Bosnians were losing their minds because they'd beaten the group leaders to keep their qualification hopes alive and the Welsh were hysterical because they'd qualified.

Since that incredible night talk has turned to who, in terms of Welsh managers, should be thanked for this incredible achievement. Should it be Coleman? Should it be Speed? Should it be Toshack? Of course all of them should be thanked. The noise in the stadium was the perfect tribute to all three men. Players had been brought into the team by Toshack. Belief, passion and professionalism had been instilled in them by Speed. And all of that and more had been galvanised by Coleman. This achievement had been an exceptionally longtime coming, but now that it had finally arrived everyone was going to enjoy it. No-one would ever remember this night for the defeat.

The reaction on social media summed up the occasion brilliantly, with some of the most relevant tweets, or at least those that are appropriate to be re-published, listed below:

Mark Pitman (UEFA Welsh Football Correspondent): The first day of a new dawn for @FAWales. An achievement that will change football in Wales more than anything before #TogetherStronger

Wayne Jones (Supporter): Toshack laid the foundations… Speed made us believe… Coleman made us achieve #TogetherStronger#France2016

Huw Davies (FourFourTwo Managing Editor): For Speedo, who began this dream. On #MentalHealthDay I cannot think of anything more fitting. Please learn more. We are always better with you.

Rob Phillips (BBC Radio Wales): What a way to do it! Not exactly according to the script but history won't remember this defeat – Welsh football will never be the same again!

Dafydd Pritchard (BBC Wales Sport): FT Bosnia 2–0 Wales. How gloriously, maddeningly Welsh to make history in such farcical fashion. Wild, cathartic celebrations here in Zenica.

Neville Southall (Wales' record cap holder): Well done to a great guy and his brilliant lads. Now go and try and win it. Fantastic, historical night. So proud!

If it had all come full circle for Chris Coleman, it had also come full circle for the fans who had travelled to all sorts of distant cities and stadiums to watch their idols and for the journalists who had made the same trips, writing wonderful words when it was all going well, as well as being optimistic when things were looking bleak. Everyone had been on a journey together and now here was their reward. Together Stronger – could anyone have picked two words more poignant?

It was especially moving to see Bryn Law of Sky Sports News celebrating the occasion so vividly. Bryn was trying manfully to maintain his professionalism on the touchline during the game, but once Cyprus went 2–1 up and maintained that lead even he couldn't help but grin. As soon as fans became aware of Cyprus' lead, they started singing, 'Bryn Law, what's the score? Bryn Law, Bryn Law, what's the score?' He could only respond with a beaming smile, throwing his arms up in celebration as he signified 2–1 with his hands. Like everyone else, he was a coiled spring waiting for the full-time whistle to blow so he could enjoy it properly. What a perfect way for his journey covering Wales to go. In 2011 he had famously broken down while speaking live on Sky Sports News following the passing of his good friend Gary Speed. Now here he was with his name being chanted by the fans, revelling in Wales' greatest moment.

Perhaps the most stirring, emotive moment of all, though, came when the squad had realised they'd done it. After the full-time whistle, still unaware of the situation, the players all wandered around the pitch completing the usual formalities, looking deflated after defeat. Coleman marched around shaking everyone's hand – standard stuff. But then the penny dropped and this exhausted bunch of players and coaches suddenly exploded with excitement. They sprinted towards their most loyal of supporters, before sliding on their stomachs across what might now be considered hallowed turf. Many of the players had been to hell and back throughout their Wales careers and they were going to revel in this historic moment with the fans. These were life-changing moments for everyone involved, the players dancing around with flags, the fans climbing the fence at the front of their section to try and get a bit closer to their heroes. It was pouring with rain but anyone with any Welsh blood in them in Zenica was having the night of their lives.

One of the greatest gestures of all came from one of the players. As the squad lined up for a team photo in the middle of the pitch – something tangible to mark the achievement of this epic milestone – Wales full-back Neil Taylor told the photographers and everyone to turn around so that the fans could be in the picture as well. They'd all been in it together, from start to finish, and now everyone had a photograph to remind them. An honourable mention must also go to Joe Ledley, who provided the perfect dance moves to commemorate the occasion; the self-proclaimed best dancer of the group, living up to his name.

Obviously the players and the fans couldn't stay in that stadium all night, although I'm sure they would have done if they could. There was still one more game to go in Cardiff before this historic campaign could be brought to a close. The players, coaches and everyone involved with the set-up had all definitely earned the right to celebrate – some of the pictures on Instagram and Twitter afterwards demonstrated just how much it all meant to everyone involved – but before the squad could go and get on with that, they spoke to the media. Here's what just two of them had to say:

Chris Coleman: 'I've never been so happy to lose 2–0. Obviously when we were walking off I saw our supporters were singing, and then it was whispered in my ear that Israel had lost so… game on after that! The team spirit of this group is incredible… they're one Welsh team that has gone that extra yard so they are special. Now you can call them the golden generation, they've earnt it and they deserve it, all of them. Now they can go back to Cardiff, puff their chests out and really enjoy the night. It's going to be a full-house in Cardiff, the celebrations will be fantastic and we want to go out with a bang. We want to enjoy it. We're going to have a nice evening tonight and enjoy it. I'll be raising a glass to my good friend Gary Speed, obviously no longer with us but always in our thoughts, in my thoughts.'

Aaron Ramsey: 'I'm over the moon, so proud of this team and of what we've achieved. Hopefully we've made the whole nation proud – it was a dream come true when that final whistle came because this is what we've always wanted to do, get the team to a major championship and finally we've achieved that. I knew we had half a chance with five minutes to go because I saw it on the board going across that Cyprus were winning. We did all the hard work before this game, got ourselves into a great position. This is definitely up there with the greatest achievements in my career, we're not a massive nation but we're a nation with a lot of players hungry for success and hopefully we can stay at this level now. We've had some really low times but we've stuck together as a team and grinded out results, getting better as the years have gone by.'

Those who had made the trip to Bosnia to watch the game would undoubtedly be suffering as a result of their celebrations there all the way until the game against Andorra on Tuesday in Cardiff, where they could do it all over again. For the fans at home, who hadn't been in Zenica, it must have felt like they had missed out on one of the best nights ever, and so Tuesday couldn't come quick enough. Whereas Bosnia had been a truly unforgettable moment for the select few who were able to travel out, Wales vs Andorra in Cardiff was for everyone, the 'I was there' moment that those in attendance would tell anyone who'd listen about for years to come.

I don't know what was different in the pre-match press conference. Perhaps it was the relief, the achievement sinking in, the pride, or a mix of all of it, but it felt totally different to any of the others that had come before it in this campaign. While Ashley Williams and Chris Coleman were totally professional as usual, and as in-sync as they had been since day one, Coleman's conference was very light-hearted. Taking a question about how he reflected on his tough times as Wales boss now he was the man who'd got Wales to a major championship, Coleman responded coolly. 'I think most people will look at what we've achieved from a footballing point of view,' he said, 'where they'll say this is the greatest Wales team in history, and I was the man in charge. Certain people who don't like me will look at it and try and water me down. Some people get carried away and build me up saying I'm this and I'm that when I'm actually not. I don't think I'm fantastic, I don't think I've reinvented football or the way I've coached has been revolutionary, I'm not one of these new-age coaches with one of these big plans. It's simply been hard work, we've had a bit of luck, great determination, great players and we've put a lot of work in so I don't really get that carried away. I'm extremely proud that I'm the manager and maybe next week when I'm at home I might look back at everything and feel slightly differently but I don't think I'm anything special.'

Ashley Williams on the other hand completely disagreed, saying Coleman's impact had been indescribable to anyone but those who had been in the training camps. He also placed the emphasis on Wales as a football nation not wasting what had been achieved. 'It's an important message we need to send out,' said Williams. 'It's taken so long and so much effort to qualify but it isn't job done. It's the start of something else now and we need to keep going now and keep qualifying for tournaments. It would be a shame to feel that this is all we wanted to achieve as a group. We need to make sure that this is the start of good things... and put things in place now to ensure it continues to happen.' Coleman echoed this, saying that he felt it was his duty going forward to 'rattle some cages' in order to make sure that people didn't get too comfortable and that Wales kept striving to achieve more. These were exceptionally encouraging words to be hearing.

If Belgium at home had been a spectacle, then the final group game against Andorra would in some respects be like a carnival. Before the game there was so much going on: there was a huge fanzone, there were commemorative T-shirts, scarves and face painting. The Super Furry Animals were playing a mini set on the pitch, Zombie Nation was practically on a loop on the PA system – all this stuff had happened at games before, but this time it just felt different, like a victory parade almost. Clappers were again attached to the seats for the Welsh fans to have yet another way to add to the atmosphere. This time, though, they included a message from Ashley Williams on the back, thanking them for creating an 'incredible' atmosphere and for their constant 'fantastic support' throughout Wales' journey. The 33,000 Welsh fans certainly appreciated the gesture, but they had one more gift to give their champions as they took to the pitch against Andorra in the last game of the campaign, and what a beautiful one it was.

With tifos proving a big hit in the home games against Belgium and Israel, the FAW had something special lined up for this final fixture and they couldn't have made a better choice. Those getting to the ground early could see the tifo laid out on the seats before anyone had come in to meddle with it, and it looked special, though nowhere near as remarkable as it looked when it was time for the anthems. It doesn't matter where you go to watch a football game or sample these incredible atmospheres: The Yellow Wall, La Bombonera, The Kop, The Maracanã, wherever – I, and 32,999 others, wouldn't have swapped our seats in the Cardiff City Stadium for anywhere in the world that night, particularly when the anthems were being played. Moments before kick-off, up it went, the tifo, and there, glistening under the floodlights on a cold autumn's night, was the Welsh flag flying high as the Welsh national anthem was thundered out by one of the most fanatical and passionate groups of fans in World football.

Seeing the dragon adorning the Canton Stand and seeing tens of thousands of its most loyal followers belting out its anthem was perfection personified – it doesn't get any better than that moment. The dragon was roaring again. It had taken a while to do so, but now it had started again no-one ever wanted it to stop. The tifo lasted a minute or two, but that moment would forever be imprinted into the memories of the people who were there to witness it. It was by far the most beautiful moment of the campaign for this supporter. Wales had suffered, believed and achieved on the way to this place they found themselves in before kick-off against Andorra, as the memories of 58 years of misery and near-misses all found itself being washed away slowly by the realisation of what Wales had accomplished.

Even the game itself against Andorra was perfect, symbolic almost of the journey that Wales had been on to get to this point. It wasn't pretty at times, stopping and starting and dealing with injuries, with Wales having to persist and persevere while being frustrated in trying to go about their business, but ultimately coming out of it deserved victors. The fans were amazing yet again, putting the anthem to one side immediately after kick-off and singing about more or less every player in their turn: 'Viva Gareth Bale, they said we had no chance, now we're off to France, Viva Gareth Bale', 'Ain't nobody like Joe Ledley', 'Hal, Robson, Hal Robson-Kanu', it went on and on before reverting to another spontaneous a cappella rendition of the anthem and then the cycle started all over again. Just a symphony of appreciation and love for the team and the incredible journey they'd been on.

The appreciation for Robson-Kanu before and during this game seemed to go into overdrive, and rightly so as the forward had been exceptional for Wales throughout the campaign. Tasked with holding up the play on a number of occasions, HRK's tireless running and persistent pestering of opposition defenders had really been vital to Wales' success. T-shirts with the words 'Dim Hal, Dim Hwyl' (No Hal, No Fun), a tongue-in-cheek reference to the 'No Pirlo, No Party' T-shirts that have become famous in recent years, were proving a huge hit and the hashtag #DimHalDimHwyl was something that Welsh football fans used regularly before and since that game. Another indicator of how loved he is by the fans was the collective groan when he went off injured in this game's early stages.

Finishing with over 80 per cent of the possession, 30 shots at the Andorran goal and 13 corners won, Wales were rampant on their way to a 2–0 victory. Aaron Ramsey deservedly got the first goal, as he would put in an outstanding performance against the European minnows, causing them all sorts of problems with his movement, trickery and range of passing. While the goal itself was unspectacular, lashing home a rebound from Ashley Williams' saved header, the celebration would prove to be exactly the opposite. The Wales midfielder led all of his teammates to the dugout, where they grabbed Joe Ledley. Huddled together, they recreated the bearded midfielder's dance moves that had famously been on display in Bosnia. It was another fantastic display of the togetherness within the squad, with a touch of humour thrown in there too.

Gareth Bale doubled Wales' lead with five minutes to go. His awesome header and free kick in Andorra 13 months ago had saved Wales' campaign from being over before it had begun, but this finish for Wales' final goal of the campaign was a simple one. There was a predatory move to latch onto a ball played loosely across the box before he struck it inside the far post to put Wales 2–0 up.

The full-time whistle was blown on this excellent, historic campaign, but with smiles all around it wasn't over yet. There was one more big show of appreciation to come from the players to their adoring fans. After retreating to the tunnel for a few minutes to catch their breath, the players were called one-by-one to return to the pitch and take their place on a stage that had been assembled in the centre circle. Each one of them, wearing T-shirts saying 'Diolch #TogetherStronger. We've made history. Together.' (Diolch being Welsh for thank you.) From Gareth Bale to Tom Lawrence – who had performed excellently having come on as a second-half substitute in this game against Andorra – each player was treated to rapturous applause and cheers from the Welsh faithful for the part they'd played in making their wildest dream come true.

On the stage champagne was sprayed. Zombie Nation was played and the squad ran over to the Canton End, diving on the floor along the way, to celebrate, sing and dance in front of all of the fans there, before going on a well-deserved lap of honour. The game and everything that surrounded it had proved a perfect way to end the campaign. I don't think anyone would have changed a thing. The crowd eventually drifted away safe in the knowledge that Wales had found their way back to where they were always meant to be. All the talk about the near-misses and the disappointments could stop now. This qualification, and everything the squad had endured and overcome in the years building up to it, was Wales' biggest success and they could rejoice in that fact.

Here is what the manager and some of the players had to say after the game:

Chris Coleman: 'There's no feeling like this. It's brilliant when you can thank these fans in the best way. We'll never ever forget the feelings we had tonight at the end. Credit to the staff, they're absolutely fantastic – this doesn't happen if you don't have a good team, and we've got a great team of people here. I think in the draw it would be nice if we escaped playing against the home nations. It'd be nice to play somebody not from the same island as us but we'll take whatever comes our way. We're very confident in ourselves, not out of arrogance, we're just confident in what we can achieve. It's not about sitting back and taking a breath thinking it's OK because we've got to France now. It's only worthwhile if we go into the tournament and have a real go at it. The goal is getting out of the group and if we do that then we can say it was worth going. It's pointless going there and falling flat on our faces. It's not about going there and saying we got there, it's about going there and competing, it's all to look forward to.'

Aaron Ramsey: 'I know Gary Speed would be looking down somewhere now on a fantastic set-up that he started in the first place. It was always going to be difficult for Chris Coleman to come in early on but he's done an unbelievable job to take over in the circumstances that he did and to finally achieve something special with this country, it's a great achievement to him and his staff and hopefully he can have many successful years with us. We don't just want to rest on this now. We've come so far, we've really worked hard together as a team and this hopefully will just be the start of Wales being competitive year after year.'

Jonny Williams: 'Nights like this you work for, so I'm delighted to be a part of it. It's been a long year for me so to be a part of this squad and part of this achievement, after losing 2–0 to Belgium in the last campaign, then Serbia and seemingly going on a downward spiral it was almost a case of where do we go from here. But to be here now, three years later, having qualified for the Euros it is hard to describe.

You can see from the celebrations how much it means to everyone, especially the manager. All praise goes to him for keeping his faith in himself and keeping the squad together. It's a huge pleasure to be a part of this.'

To a Wales fan these few days were pretty much perfect. I wouldn't even change the defeat to Bosnia because it was symbolic in the sense that, for once, luck had gone our way with Cyprus doing Wales a favour and helping seal qualification early. It had been such an epic adventure for everyone, not least the supporters twice or three times my age who had waited a lifetime to see Wales qualify. How on earth could anything top this? Going to France and achieving another incredible feat would be a start. With everything that had happened to Wales over the years who would bet against them doing something spectacular there?

Regardless of what happened at Euro '16, Wales had already secured some of their biggest victories on the way to France and could be immensely proud – not just in terms of results, but in terms of the immense effect they'd had on a nation of people who'd stuck with them through thick and thin. They'd filled the stadiums to the rafters; thousands of dragons had flown across Europe to follow their heroes to some of the furthest corners of the continent; the spontaneous renditions of the national anthem during that Belgium home game – absolutely amazing dedication. The way the team had come together as a group to be considered one of the best teams in the world, not just in terms of chemistry but in terms of rankings too – unbelievable. Was there another national team that had achieved what this incredible group had done over the last few years?

Being a part of this journey as a fan has been maddening, challenging and difficult at times, but sticking by them the entire time to get to this point led to the most glorious feeling any Welsh football fan has ever felt. Every real football fan will love this story – whether you look at the last 60 years in the round or the last ten years or so in isolation, Wales overcame all odds and expectations. Everybody loves the story of Spain and their epic run to three major tournament wins in a row, the story of Germany and their resurgence, the stories of football gods like Messi and Ronaldo, but this story is up there with all of them – surpassing them in my opinion. It is more than just a football story, it's a story of a community, and how that community endured and developed in the face of almost every challenge the world could throw at it, including the tragic loss of one of its icons – Gary Speed.

Memories of Speed's career, and the man he was, will forever go hand-in-hand with the memories of this historic campaign and the work done by his best friend, Chris Coleman, to see every Welshman's dream – not least Speed's – realised. This is no time for Toshack to be left out of the picture, either. Toshack had a big part to play in this success; if he hadn't have had such faith in the youngsters then they could not have developed in the way they did. They'd have undoubtedly come through, but would they have come through so early and had so many caps without Toshack? The fans know that he had an immense impact, and Toshack knew himself that his successors would see the benefits of his work, although both of the men that came in after him put in an absurd amount of work themselves.

Coleman, or Sir Chris as some fans have started calling him, showed unbelievable courage to come in and lead the side in incomprehensibly difficult circumstances. His reward was the honour of leading the team, his team – some of the most extraordinary, fierce, hungry footballers ever to kick a ball – back into battle on one of football's biggest stages.

It was one hell of a ride: fate, blind luck, fortune (which does favour the brave, after all), they all came to Wales' aid to help them find their way back to the zenith of international football. But at the end of the day what saw Wales accomplish this amazing achievement was their never-say-die attitude. That incredible spirit that you can only find in the British Isles, Wales embodied that spirit so well throughout this journey – when some of their bodies were broken, even in this campaign, these players, coaches and fans' incredible spirit and determination to see their country return to where it belongs saw them through and they've all had their just desserts. Wales has done it, and the sky is the limit going forward.

Vive les Gallois! Long live the Welsh!

Standings after Matchdays 9 & 10

Pos.	Team	GP	W	D	L	F	A	GD	Pts
1	Belgium (Q)	10	7	2	1	24	5	19	23
2	Wales (Q)	10	6	3	1	11	4	7	21
3	Bosnia (P)	10	5	2	3	17	12	5	17
4	Israel	10	4	1	5	16	14	2	13
5	Cyprus	10	4	0	6	16	17	- 1	12
6	Andorra	10	0	0	10	4	36	- 32	0

Matchday 9 results:
Bosnia & Herzegovina 2–0 Wales
Andorra 1–4 Belgium
Israel 1–2 Cyprus

Matchday 10 results:
Wales 2–0 Andorra
Belgium 3–1 Israel
Cyprus 2–3 Bosnia & Herzegovina

CHAPTER 16

Wales' next (best?) crop of talent

'Chris Coleman and others speak about this being the
Golden Generation, and I think they're wrong personally.
The Golden Generation will be the next one.'

CHRIS WHITLEY, CHAIRMAN FAW INTERNATIONAL BOARD

AFTER THE BOSNIA game, the 58-year wait was over. The
country's name would soon feature in the draw for the finals of
a major tournament. Having made history by qualifying for
a major tournament for the first time since 1958, the next
challenge for Wales was to create a situation where they
could do it again, and again and again. With the experience
of having qualified, doing it again shouldn't be beyond
the realms of expectation. Wales had qualified in spite of
constant injuries and other distractions. The draw had not
been easy. If Wales could get past this group, they can surely
do it again. Managing the mentality and the mind-set away
from the pitch shouldn't be a problem going into any future
campaigns. With young players like George Williams already
blooded on the international stage, now would seem an apt
moment to examine Wales' plans to ensure they have the
best possible talent available on the pitch in generations to
come, as we take a look at the youth development set-up.

The most important word here is opportunity. There have
to be opportunities for those kids, who practise every day and
who live for football, to come and strut their stuff for Wales at
youth level, a pathway if you will. Wales' player development
programme has undergone quite a transformation since
the turn of the millennium in particular, and the Welsh

Football Trust has put in an incredible amount of work to ensure that. Structure is key here, because there was a pathway previously, but the organisation of it has improved dramatically in the last ten years or so, due to a number of factors.

The first of these developments was the formation of Welsh Premier League academies, which assisted a number of youngsters in moving on to better clubs much earlier in their careers, or at least attaining a better quality of football on a weekly basis, as opposed to simply playing arranged fixtures periodically throughout the season. Another has been streamlining the transition between the Wales youth teams. It has been mentioned previously how complicated the relationships are between different parts of the Wales set-up, and reshuffling all of that has been key, right up to the 2012 FAW strategy we looked at earlier.

But in terms of improving the pathway it all started to snowball during John Toshack's tenure, as a clearer connection was made between the under-16s and the intermediate groups. Previously the under-16s would come underneath the school structure when Toshack was running the team, but in 2008 the Trust took over responsibility for that team which, after an initial period of transition, embedded itself into the Trust and the way they operated the other youth teams. This then enabled Osian Roberts to develop and introduce a structure to Gary Speed, when he came in as manager, that saw a seamless transition through the age groups, right up to the under-21s and the first team. It was also significant in a financial sense for the development of those youth teams because, although the Schools FA had run the under-15s/16s and under-18s in their hundred-year history, everyone who worked for that association did so on a voluntary basis and, as a body, had a maximum of £25,000 every year to spend on those squads. A stark contrast to the 40 full-time staff that the Trust can dedicate to any given task, and the significantly greater budget that comes with it.

It cannot be stressed enough how important Osian Roberts is to all of this. Many of the people I've spoken to about the way youth development has changed within Welsh football have highlighted how influential he has been. Roberts has been hailed previously as the most powerful man in Welsh football, certainly his involvement in pretty much everything that Wales do in football would suggest that. See some of his roles for example: technical director at the Welsh Football Trust, manager of the under-16s, leading, structuring and developing Wales' coach education courses, coaching and becoming assistant manager for the senior team in recent years. Of course, these things wouldn't run without the people around Roberts, regardless of whether he is there or not, and the FAW are very much to thank for creating that structure around him that has enabled him to flourish. But his importance to each and every facet of Welsh football, particularly on the youth development side, is immeasurable.

Speak to any of the current youth prospects, or youngsters who have recently made the jump to the first team, and they'll tell you how important Roberts has been to it all. The fact that Roberts is involved at the start and the end of the Wales player pathway is ideal for every player involved, as he can develop each of them individually and manage their individual pathways through the game. Gus Williams, talent identification manager for the Welsh Football Trust, who is one of the hardest working people within the Trust and knows of every Welsh player of any age group, hailed Roberts' work with Speed as a key point in the development of youth football in Wales. 'It has certainly changed since Osian became a coach with Gary Speed,' explains Williams. 'The interaction is far greater than it was at any other stage before that point. That was the commencement of a better approach to youth development, a marriage of organisations, combining for the good of youth development and all having an understanding of what youth development did and should look like in Wales moving forward into the future. The difference was clear in those early days but since then, there's been a far greater emphasis on making the base of the pyramid far stronger to ensure the top benefits from it in the long run.'

Finding the talent is obviously the biggest challenge. In years gone by there have been stories of some players being recommended to the scouts by fans, as opposed to the scouts in Wales simply knowing about these players and their talents. That doesn't happen any more as the set-up is so comprehensive – Wales now have 20 scouts across the UK, working predominantly in the under-11 to under-16 age groups, and they're out every weekend looking at players, writing reports, collecting data on who's the next big thing and who needs to be scouted further. It's all about communication and having the right people in the right places, building relationships as you go along. The Welsh Football Trust is in contact with all 92 professional clubs in England, the Conference clubs, the Welsh Premier League clubs, and have recently started to roll out into Scotland, where they have already found an eligible player that has caught the eye – there's a young Welshman playing in AC Milan too who is on the radar by all accounts. So you can see how far things have come from the point of ten to 15 years ago where Wales were missing players on their own doorstep, to the point where they're finding them on the continent. There has just been an immense change in youth football in Wales. There's now a plan, a formalised scouting network, a coaching syllabus, a structured player pathway – everything has come on so much in such a short space of time and really bodes well for the future.

Dragon Park has played a huge role in all of this, too, the home of Welsh football that was developed in 2013 and opened by the then-UEFA president Michel Platini, after securing funding from UEFA to help Wales build the vision they had for football in the country. For those fortunate enough to work within the Trust, it is a huge motivating factor coming to work every morning in a modern, fully-equipped, fully-resourced facility – it assists your work greatly. It's also a selling point when you're trying to bring players and coaches into the Welsh set-up. They see that Wales has this modern facility at its disposal with everything that the modern game requires integrated within.

UEFA have done an awful lot to help developing countries, in a footballing sense, to realise their full potential, something that goes somewhat overlooked in the media. What they do is they arrange study visits for nations of similar population, geographical size and so on, to visit each other and observe the way these different countries go about laying out their footballing landscapes. The Wales set-up in particular has visited countries like Holland, Belgium, Denmark and Norway, learning the dos and don'ts in terms of what each country wants to do going forward, collecting ideas. Again, though, the biggest thing with anything like this is giving it time to develop. Belgium had a ten-year plan to reach the World Cup finals and they achieved it, but only through patience and perseverance from all involved in Belgian football – supporters, players, coaches, the lot. Wales are now starting to see their plan realise its potential, but there is still work to do. The key thing is to stick to the plan.

There is plenty of evidence that the plan is working, particularly with the under-16s recently winning the Victory Shield outright for the first time since 1948/49, before retaining it for a second year. There have been positive results in other campaigns as well, but with success comes more expectation. What has been achieved so far is short-term success, but the Trust and the FAW won't rest on their laurels – this will only inspire them to attain long-term success. The challenge is doing that with the same financial resources you had before, because the expectation is going to be for this success to increase without much more money to play with. So all you can do is try and be more innovative about your work while trying to foresee what challenges might face the game in the future, and plan accordingly to combat those. Regional development centres are now being discussed, for the north and south of

Wales, to try and give as many opportunities as possible to those kids who dream of pulling on the red shirt one day. The psychological aspect seems well covered, and that will surely be a challenge – getting these players ready psychologically at a younger age for the challenges that they are going to face at senior level. But everyone believes in the vision and the way forward looks very bright for Welsh football. It's all about realising that potential for the next generation now.

For an insight into how the youth development set-up is working right now from a player's perspective, I spoke to West Brom's Tyler Roberts about his experiences within it. Roberts qualifies for Wales through his grandparents. Having captained Wales' under-16s to their first outright Victory Shield win since 1949, and being labelled as having the potential to be the best Wales Number 9 since Mark Hughes, there's obviously a lot of expectation that he could be a fantastic player in the future. Before I spoke to him, not long after he'd trained with the senior squad before the Belgium home game, the then 16 year old had never taken part in an interview about his football career. Here's what he had to say:

JT: It seems like an obvious place to start, but how highly do you think of the Wales youth set-up?
TR: When we go away it's completely different than being at your club – different people, a different way of working, different practice. Training is more specific to an opposition with your national team than it is with a club team, because you have much less time to get ready but it's a good break to go away and it's a good change of pace. I know a few players in other youth set-ups and we talk about the banter and how different it is; what different kind of things we do when we go away to play for our countries. It's difficult to tell how the Welsh set-up might compare to other set-ups just by talking to my teammates at club level, but the Welsh set-up is good. They have a good structure, good coaches, they're improving at every age group, taking real steps forward. Wales is a proud country and I'm proud to be part of it. It's a good set-up to be a part of, especially being captain.

JT: How early on do you get taught Wales' style and what are your thoughts on it – is it a kind of football you like?

TR: We were taught the style of play almost immediately when I first joined. I must have been in the under-13s when it all started. We were being pushed to play out of the back and play through the thirds. I like that style of play, playing through the thirds suits the forwards too, because when we get it in the middle there's a chance for forwards to run in behind or pull short and get the ball to feet, so it makes us less predictable as a team and harder to handle. The player education is good. We do a lot of work in the video analysis room, looking at the other team, what they're good at, what we can exploit. I think against England in the Victory Shield we just focused on the fact that they like to push forward in numbers, so on the counter we knew there would be spaces to get in behind them and get a goal.

JT: Touching on England, you kicked off that victorious Victory Shield campaign last year (2014) against them. What are your recollections of that game and the campaign on the whole?

TR: We knew before the game if we could get something, or even win, it would be a massive moment and we could actually win the Victory Shield for Wales. In the game they had a lot of possession, we just tried to grind it out and keep working. The desire in our team got us through that game and when we got the goal the reaction was amazing, which shows how much it meant to us. The biggest aim was to get the Victory Shield, to win that; we did and I'm very proud of that, but playing in all of those games was a great experience because they're all such good tests.

JT: Have you enjoyed being a captain, and how do you deal with the expectations or comparisons that are being made of you at such a young age?

TR: Leading by example is what it's all about. On the pitch, communicating with the players, pushing them through the game, definitely in the England game, just to keep us all focusing on the task at hand is what it's all about. I've really enjoyed being captain. It's a great feeling walking out and leading the team. Very special.

On that type of level, I take the expectations and comparisons in my stride. It doesn't make me big-headed nor do I dwell on it too much, it's just a nice compliment to be compared to such great players. Last season I came into the year adamant that it was going to be a good season for me. With hard work and doing that extra bit you can get there and do something special. It has surprised me how far I've been able to come in the last year to a degree; starting off the season in the under-16s and then getting a call-up to the senior squad.

JT: Some say that your team now has the potential to be better than the current squad. Do you feel that?
TR: I think we've got a strong team with some great players, especially going into the Euros having just won the Victory Shield. I don't think it has happened too often where an under-17s Wales side has reached the final stages of a European Championship tournament so hopefully we can do that. I think all of the team is good. We've got a strong base in defence, with the likes of Cole Dasilva from Chelsea, the midfield is very strong with people from Manchester City like Matty Smith, Ben Woodburn from Liverpool, and the attack this year has looked particularly strong.

JT: How important have Chris Coleman and Osian Roberts been to your development?
TR: It makes you feel much more comfortable seeing a face that you know and can talk to. Osian helped me integrate and introduced me to the players. Having him at under-16s is key, because he knows what is expected of senior players and can develop us at that early level accordingly, which is a very good thing. He's a great manager. I think he'll be pushing on in a few years for a job in a managerial post, maybe at a club, maybe for Wales. I met Chris Coleman for the first time at the Wales–Bosnia game in October. I met him before the game and he just told me if you're good enough, you're old enough which is very good to hear. If I were called up it would be a great achievement in my career, a great honour. I'm sure my granddad would be proud. It gives me hope definitely to see Jordan Williams called up recently, and also

with Harry Wilson getting his debut so young back against Belgium, it's something to aspire to.

JT: How much of an insight was it for you to be involved before the Belgium home game?
TR: The technical side of the game was the most striking thing in terms of differences: every first touch has to be good, every pass has to be clean. In terms of people to learn from, as an attacker, Gareth Bale is of course a great one to look at and learn a lot of lessons from, but in general I think the one I learnt the most from was Joe Allen. He was very good at knowing where the space was and thinking three steps ahead of everyone else on the pitch. I'd be very proud to be involved again, but having been there before now, I'd be more comfortable and able to express myself a bit more.

It speaks wonders for both the youth prospects like Tyler Roberts, and for the set-up itself, that at such a young age he has such a clear understanding of where he is in his development, where he could be and what is going to get him to the senior level. Speaking with such maturity at such a young age in his first interview says an awful lot for both him and the set-up that has unearthed him and nurtured him. The brilliant thing is that Roberts isn't the only one who displays these qualities; there's a plethora of talent coming through the ranks that are cut from exactly the same cloth, and it is the result of years and years of hard work behind the scenes by so many people that has seen the youth development set-up in Wales end up where it is now.

With Jonny Williams and Emyr Huws – two exceptional talents – missing so many games through injury, the Euro '16 campaign perhaps did not see the youth players get as many chances. But there's no doubt they are good enough to be in that team. Tom Lawrence has been in the squad for every game, the former Manchester United youngster looking a bright prospect up front in years to come. George Williams has looked great when he's come in. A midfield of Emyr Huws,

Jonny Williams, Jordan Williams and George Williams is very strong, and with a duo like Harry Wilson and Tom Lawrence, or even Tyler Roberts up top, then there is certainly a lot to be excited about in years to come. Adam Henley, Adam Matthews and Paul Dummett are great prospects at the back too, with Danny Ward in goal certainly one for the future. This group of players is pacey, powerful, gutsy, and they all have good football brains – if it wasn't for the immense talent of the senior players, then these players would certainly be starting more often. Make no mistake, when they do get their opportunity, these youngsters will live up to the hype and continue the current crop's trailblazing tendencies long into the future.

Chapter 17

A word from 'Sir Chris', ahead of the tournament we've waited generations for

'Enjoy every minute of it. Get excited. We're not going to France to enjoy the experience, we'll enjoy the experience if we perform and make the nation proud of our performances.'

Chris Coleman, Wales manager

We've waited an awful long time, a lifetime for most of us, to be able to say it's time to hear from the national team manager who led our country to a major international tournament. After Wales' 3–2 friendly defeat to Holland in November 2015, I got the chance to sit down and have a chat with the man himself, Chris Coleman. Here is what he had to say:

JT: It's been a few weeks now since Wales qualified. We've all waited a long time for this, but have all of the emotions that come with that success been everything you expected?
CC: The first couple of days afterwards it hadn't sunk in, but a week or two down the line it hit me, and it was unbelievable. If I'm honest, I've immediately switched my focus to the tournament, the possibilities of who we might play, where we need to stay, what we need to do when we get there, but you never move on from it. I say that in the sense that you never forget what's happened and what you've achieved, but you have to move on quite quickly in terms of how you're going to plan going forward. Every time I think about it I get goose bumps. Thinking about what we've done, it's an amazing feeling, the best feeling I've had in football for sure.

JT: Looking back to when you took over from Gary Speed, it was clear how conflicted you were in taking the role, but how do you reflect on that period and the challenges you had to overcome?

CC: In those first few months of the World Cup campaign, where we were losing, we were being heavily criticised; I was being heavily criticised; a lot of the criticism of me was justified really. If you're not doing what you believe in, you can't complain when people criticise you for failing, but I wasn't ready to change what Speed had been doing. When I first came in I was told, even before I got the job, that the FAW didn't want to change anything because what Speed had been doing was working – which I could understand, in some ways – so I didn't want to betray a trust and I obviously didn't want to betray Speeds. I promise you though, had Speeds been around he would have said to me – he probably would have torn a strip off of me – 'What are you doing? Do it your own way. Don't do it my way, stand up for what you believe in.' And he probably would have given me what for. But I wasn't ready to do what I wanted to do. That came to a head against Serbia away. I knew it wasn't working. I wasn't enjoying the job, because I wasn't doing what I believed in. The players maybe weren't believing in me because I wasn't believing in myself. That was the line in the sand.

I came back and spent a lot of time with Ian Gwyn Hughes [FAW head of public affairs and close friend of Coleman's]. He told me I had to do what I thought was right, my partner at the time said the same, that I wasn't enjoying it, that I was doing it all wrong and that I was wasting a huge opportunity, because I wasn't doing what I believed in. That was when I knew I had to make some big decisions, and changed everything really, but even in the rest of the campaign it was a case of one step forward, one step back and it got to the stage where I wondered if the FAW wanted to give me another crack at it. I wanted another crack at it, because I thought the experience we all had in the first campaign would stand us in good stead, but it was an uncertain period – thankfully, we all agreed on giving it another go.

JT: When you spoke after Serbia, it was as if you'd known that the changes that followed that game needed to happen and you'd known that for a long time. is that a fair assessment?

CC: Speeds said, when they won five games out of six, two of the last three were qualifying games with nothing riding on them and one was a friendly, and he said himself: 'Forget what we've done. We've won some games with no pressure on us. Don't judge us now, judge us on the next campaign,' which was typical of Speeds really. I thought, for us to play the way we want to play with the ball, we've got to learn to be better without it. We've got to be more streetwise, more cynical without the ball and we've got to be stronger in our decision-making.

You always have to build from the base, upwards – it doesn't work the other way. If you build a strong roof and you don't have the foundations in place, there's only one thing that's going to happen, so we had to build the other way to what we had been. I saw that in the first campaign. Some of the games we played really well, really good football and we lost. If we were going to qualify, it wasn't going to be that way, just concentrating on how good we are with the ball, it was going to come down to whether or not we were good enough to win 1–0, mentally strong enough to hold on to a 1–0, or tactically sharp enough to go away to somewhere hostile and hold on to a result. That's what we concentrated on, we never took anything away from the players offensively, we told them to use their imagination when we had the ball, but it was when we didn't have it, in transitions, we needed to be much brighter and much harder in our thinking, and that's where the improvement came along and the results started coming in. The nation started believing and it all snowballed, but we had to do all of the horrible things to get there.

We know about the gifted players we have, what we didn't know was if we were good enough as a unit to go and do what we needed to do to qualify. We had to be careful not to give the players too much, too soon, in terms of tactics, but that's why we took the risk with Andorra away going with the 3–5–2, because we had so long to prepare for that game, time we wouldn't have to prepare before the next game against Bosnia. I had the formation in my head that was going to get us what we needed to go on and qualify, but doing it in training is nothing. We had to do it in a game, so I took a risk and did it in that game. It could have, and nearly did backfire badly, but thankfully it didn't. Then we did the same against Bosnia, and we were off and running, formation, work-rate, it was all there. We told the players they needed to be able to adapt to more than one formation, it was going to be horses for courses, depending on who we were up against, what type of game it was; sometimes it changed within the game, we've changed formation two or three times in some games, so the players became more adaptable, which is what we wanted, but we had to take that huge leap of faith against Andorra in the first game and, thankfully, it paid off.

JT: When did you first feel comfortable in the role?
CC: I still don't think I've got my feet under the table. I'd never allow myself to get to that point where I feel comfortable, because we can always be doing more. When you're manager of your country, every decision you make is scrutinised by the whole nation, so when you're making big decisions you've got to be prepared to have 100 per cent belief in them and be prepared for the consequences, good or bad. After Serbia is when I had that confidence, the confidence to say, 'You know what, whatever I see that needs changing, however I see it, I'm going to make it happen, win, lose or draw,' but I'm still not comfortable, I'd never allow myself to be.

JT: Picking up on the scrutiny you mentioned there, do you think you and the team were harshly scrutinised during that first campaign?
CC: I think certain people use it as an opportunity to jump on a bandwagon, to write a story, whatever they want, they may have a different agenda. Even now, people who were criticising us then are still criticising us now, which tells you everything about that individual and what their angle is. Some of the media that were criticising us then are now very positive and hats off to them. At that stage I was an easy target. We weren't winning, was I going to keep my job? Then I lost my passport. The big mistake I made there was saying to the team

that they should still travel out in the morning as planned, get some rest – we'd worked on everything tactically – and not to worry about me while I went and got another passport and ended up arriving just a few hours after the team did. I gave people an excuse to have a pop at me. It was a schoolboy error by me and the heat was on that time because we didn't beat Macedonia, we lost 3–0 to Serbia and it was really touch-and-go regarding my future. I was never going to leave though, especially not halfway through a campaign, and after the way the first campaign had gone I felt I had a massive point to prove.

When people were saying we should have qualified, we had an incredibly difficult group, with every team ranked higher than us – I thought it was unrealistic to think like that, but all of the excitement had come from the excellent run the team went on with Speed. It was a very tough group but, because that was such a tough campaign, it really put me in the frame of mind going into my second campaign of not bothering with what was being said by the media, ex-players. Good or bad, I didn't care, because I knew exactly what I was going to do and that I was going to stand or fall by it. At the time I didn't think the first campaign was good for me, but when we decided I was going to get another crack at it I realised how valuable it was, because it put me in the right frame of mind, a blessing probably.

JT: You made some shrewd acquisitions over the summer in preparation for this latest campaign, getting James Chester and Ian Mitchell. How and why did those moves come about?
CC: I was tipped off about James possibly qualifying for Wales through his grandparents, so I spoke to him. I called him a couple of times, couldn't get through to him, left him a message and he never got back to me, so I thought maybe he didn't want to play international football. It turns out he just had a problem with his phone, but then I tried him again and I got him, had a very positive conversation with him and I thought he'd be ideal for us, given the personnel we already have and what he offers, and he's come in and been superb. He's one of those players, he's been great on the pitch for us, but off the pitch he has been fantastic too. He's one of those fellas that is probably as good a

team player as you're ever going to get, he's all about the team. He's a great professional, he's got total respect for everybody around him, and he's been a revelation.

Ian Mitchell? There's an arrogance in football where most other sports use psychologists regularly, but in football we don't think we need that because we're the number one sport in the world, a bit like sports science when that came about. But if it's going to make you better, make you think differently, see things from a different angle, it's something worth giving a shot and I think Ian Mitchell was that little piece of the puzzle that we didn't have. The players don't always want to talk to me, or my assistants or my coaches, they want to talk to people with professional experience outside of football at times, about something other than football that is on their mind. If they can't unload then they carry that, so sometimes they need to unload about football and about their private lives. Everything else was in place, but Ian was just that key, that piece we didn't have and he's been absolutely fantastic for us.

JT: People would be interested to know how you prepare for these campaigns, especially given the formations we've played in this campaign, so could you give an insight into that side of things?
CC: It's very straightforward. We see who we draw, we work out our targets in terms of what points we need to finish where and we decide on a formation that we think would be best against each team home and away. The formations we decide on obviously depend on who is available in any given squad – it's not often we get the same squad for two international windows in a row. The last campaign we played 4–2–3–1 most games, or 4–1–4–1, we never deviated from having four at the back, it was never a three, but I'm a big fan of having three centre-backs because there are more secrets to that system, you can adjust and adapt more. In the 3–4–2–1 that we play, we've got the perfect players to play it, which means we can exploit all of the formations' strengths. In transitions, we can be very difficult to beat defensively or we can play counterattack very quickly, so that's why I like it. In the last campaign, we predominantly played with a back-four, with a holding two, or having one holding and two pushing, but we changed it for

this campaign and that's why it's more difficult now when we have pull-outs to keep this formation, because most of the players we have know it, but one or two that come in perhaps aren't as confident and that's where the doubt creeps in and we have to decide whether we can carry it onto the pitch, or if we have to change it.

JT: The support has been incredible throughout this campaign, but how strange has it been for you personally, going from being booed off against Andorra to being lauded now?

CC: That's football isn't it!? The Andorra game was the big gamble, because we'd have normally played with a more conventional formation than 3–5–2. We were on a horrendous pitch, playing against a team that were willing to do anything to avoid defeat, defend with everybody, dirty tactics, they were going to do what they needed to do and that's up to them; we knew what we were going to face. I said to the players before the game that all we needed to do was to come away with the three points to start the campaign off properly, because this was the formation that was going to carry us forward. I told them there was no pressure on them, if it didn't work it would be my fault, I was willing to take responsibility. We thought it would get a little bit edgy and nervy, because of us taking a gamble on the formation, but we didn't expect to go behind after six minutes following a dubious penalty. Then the whole feeling was, 'Here we go again, Wales off to a bad start.' So we had to fight our way back into the game, and we went in 1–1 at half-time – my message to the players was that it didn't matter how we did it, whether we scored immediately or in the last second, we were going to score again and take the three points. We weren't playing very well, but it wasn't their fault, they were learning the formation and the pitch was appalling – they just needed to stay calm and believe, and they did and we got the three points.

That game brought us all together, because of the manner of the performance and the fact that we'd got through it. The next game was Bosnia, where we used 3–5–2 again. I was lambasted for using it against Andorra, critics saying it was too negative, the players didn't know what they were doing, and so on. But because that formation was key to getting the result against Bosnia, as the players had gained that experience with it and knew a bit more about it, the trust grew further within the group, and from the fans' perspective too. When the fans were singing for my head against Macedonia, it wasn't something that bothered me. It never has. I cut myself off from it, but when you go to Brussels and you see what the fans were doing on that night, wow! That gives you an enormous nudge forward, that extra little bit of energy, that sharpness. They were singing for the players from start to finish, that's so special. When you go to Haifa, Cyprus and Bosnia, and you're seeing all of the thousands of fans going crazy, that gives you an edge to do a bit better and the players responded magnificently.

JT: You're always talking about getting the extra 1 per cent and how invaluable your backroom staff are, but how much credit do they deserve for the part they've played in this success?
CC: We've got a lot of staff! People know about some of our staff more than others. Osian for example does all sorts with the younger age groups, as well as what he does with the senior team. But fans might not know much about the likes of Ryland Morgans, who is our go-to-guy in sports science, and drew up the entire physical programme that Welsh football follows. That's his, he's at the top of his game and has been irreplaceable. Kit was massive for me, because he's someone I trust completely and you need someone like that as a manager. I was gutted when he left, but Paul Trollope has come in, who is an excellent coach, and has done very well for us since coming in after we beat Belgium. Martyn Margetson, our goalkeeping coach, does a lot of work with Wayne, Owain and Wardy and has taken responsibility for teaching the team how to defend against set-plays. We've only conceded four goals throughout the campaign so that speaks for itself really. He's been excellent. Our video analysts have been exceptional, making sure I get what I want from all of the clips to show the players – we watch a lot of games, but they never stop working for us.

Our head kit man, Dai, does 17-hour days, he puts in so much work, it's incredible. When we're on camp, he works his socks off. He's been here 15 to 20 years. One of our masseurs has been here

25 years, he's done over 100 games. These people are never seen by our supporters. Most of them won't have heard of them, but within our group they make such a difference. They do it because they love it, they're so important. Our medical team is the best in the business. We pay a lot of attention to that side of things, because we have to send players back fit so they can play the next game for us, then we build relationships with the clubs; we build trust and our medical team is crucial to that. The whole Together Stronger campaign, that's come from Ian Gwyn Hughes and Peter Barnes, people who work in the FAW office and are not necessarily with me 24/7, but everyone in that office has played their part too. They've all been crucial. Across the board, there has been a coming together, a belief, a huge push towards achieving something special, so they all deserve a pat on the back, they've all been fantastic.

JT: How much more is there to come from this team?

CC: Well, Jonny Williams and Emyr Huws missed most of the campaign, but played very well when available. George Williams missed most of the campaign through injury, but he's a very exciting young player. Tom Lawrence has just burst onto the scene. There's a good blend of talent coming through, certainly, and these boys will have something to say going forward. Everyone is going to look at France and what squad we're taking, but there's plenty more international football to come after that. There's a huge World Cup campaign and these young players are going to have a big input on that. This is very much a group of players in the ascendency. It's not like they're coming towards the end of their career and they've finally done it. They're on the rise and the sky's the limit.

It's exciting for Wales. We've got good players. There's always injuries, but the pool of players is much bigger, the quality is much better and the experience is improving every time the group comes together, too, and that's massive for Wales going forward in terms of what to expect from this team after France. In terms of the friendlies we've got to come, we're looking at top European opposition – unless Brazil or Argentina want to play us – but I'd rather lose 3–2 to a top team like Holland than beat a lesser team 3–0. I was very impressed with our performance against Holland. People say there's nothing riding on friendlies, but there's always something on it. You're best off playing a team that are going to stretch you, then you can give the younger players a feeling of what that stage is like, which we were able to do with Bale, Ramsey and Robson-Kanu out, but the younger lads did exceptionally well. Tom Lawrence got 90 minutes, George and Jonny Williams did well, Emyr Huws scored a great goal, we got a lot out of that. With the two or three friendlies to come, we've got to keep in mind what squad we want to take to France, what level they're playing at, how much football they've had – all of that will impact on who starts for us in those friendlies and who comes on to finish the game.

JT: Does the fact that you're in Pot 4 for the Euro 2016 draw protect the team from getting ahead of themselves going into France?
CC: Yes, but also we're in new territory, we've never been in this position. We had a run of one loss in 13 games, unbeaten in so many qualifiers, top ten in the rankings, and its human nature to question how we handle those expectations. Then you see the draw and we're in Pot 4. I'm sure that teams will look at Pot 4, see Wales there and want to avoid us more than they will anyone else, and they should think like that. I think also, for us to say we're not deemed as one of the big-hitters or the main threats, we're definitely better when we're up against a giant and we know we've got to be at our best. The players have enjoyed that challenge. There's no fear. It's a challenge, how far can this be taken forward, how much of an impact can we make? The message through the campaign was never to win, it was to create an identity. We needed that challenge, now it's a case of how far can we take that? We've got to concentrate on what makes us good, rather than the result, concentrate on the process of what makes us good, and stick to that, regardless of the result.

JT: Finally, the fans have heard a lot from all sorts of people in this book, but what is your message to the fans ahead of France?
CC: Enjoy every minute of it. Get excited. We're not going to France to enjoy the experience, we'll enjoy the experience if we produce, if we

perform, and we make the nation proud of our performances. That's what they should be looking for, that's what we'll be looking to do, looking to go there and make the nation proud. Get excited, enjoy it, and let's see what comes from it!'

Also from Y Lolfa:

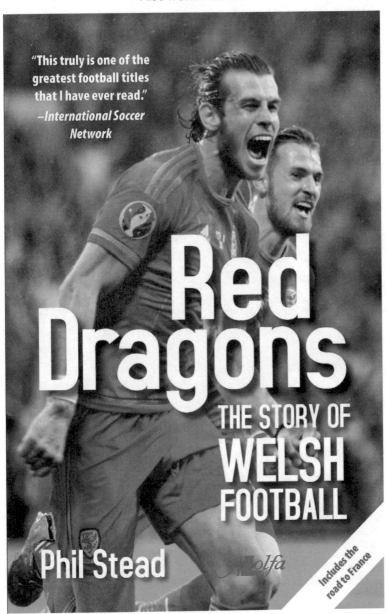

"This truly is one of the greatest football titles that I have ever read."
–International Soccer Network

Red Dragons
THE STORY OF WELSH FOOTBALL

Phil Stead

Includes the road to France

£9.99

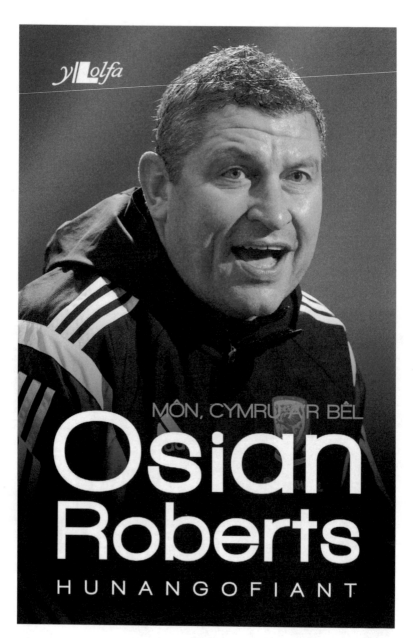

MÔN, CYMRU A'R BÊL

Osian Roberts

HUNANGOFIANT

£9.99

The Red Dragon

The story of the Welsh Flag

DIOLCH
#TogetherStronger

Siôn T. Jobbins

y lolfa

£3.99

The Dragon Roars Again is just one of a
whole range of publications from Y Lolfa.
For a full list of books currently in print, send
now for your free copy of our new full-colour
catalogue. Or simply surf into our website

www.ylolfa.com

for secure on-line ordering.

TALYBONT CEREDIGION CYMRU SY24 5HE
e-mail ylolfa@ylolfa.com
website www.ylolfa.com
phone (01970) 832 304
fax 832 782